Praise for
BETWEEN THE DARK AND THE DAYLIGHT

"Here, at last, is a book for those ready to make peace with the unsolvable riddles of present-day life. Why are we so lonely in a world of so little privacy? Why do we work so hard for control we can never achieve? Whether the problem that keeps you up at night is how to find safety in a world that is always changing or how to deal with guilt in a life that is far from perfect, Sister Joan has good news for you: these are the questions that make you human, and can make you more joyously human if you choose."

—Barbara Brown Taylor, author of *Learning to Walk in the Dark*

"The great spiritual writers knew that truth can be found most often in paradoxes and contradictions. To find light you must go through darkness. To seek knowledge you must admit that you know little. To live you must die to self. Joan Chittister's new book explores the meaning of some of the most profound spiritual paradoxes and, in the process, helps the reader find her or his way to new life. Sister Joan has long been one of my favorite spiritual writers, and with this new book she has given us more of her trademark common sense, insight, and wisdom."

—James Martin, SJ, author of *Jesus: A Pilgrimage*

"As always, Joan has put her finger and her pen to the right and needed words. She well describes those liminal spaces wherein human beings best grow and become their best selves. She could never describe them so well if she had not walked through them herself."

—Richard Rohr, OFM, founder of Center for Action and
Contemplation and author of *Falling Upward*

"This little book is an alarm clock for the spiritual journey. It wakes the reader up to the fact that our life journey is unique for each of us, yet we are twined together in the presence of God in every moment. Joan brings her years of faithful monasticism to open up the painful contradictions of our time. Wake up! The time is NOW!"

—Simone Campbell, SSS, executive director of NETWORK,
author of *A Nun on the Bus*

"Joan Chittister has written what promises to be a spiritual classic—a guide for those of us who have ever spent sleepless nights wrestling with our own frustrations, fear of the unknown, and pain of loss and separation. Through the wisdom of a woman who has experienced all of these, we learn how doubt can lead to greater clarity, hopelessness to new life, and solitude to deeper connection. In short, how the paradoxes that confound life can transform it. This is the most poetic writing yet from a woman who is a modern prophet."

—Judith Valente, author of *Atchison Blue* and correspondent for *Religion & Ethics Newsweekly* on PBS

"This book could be life-changing for many. Joan Chittister highlights the paradoxes and contradictions of life, things that we experience as obstacles, as life-denying, such as loss, confusion, doubt, failure, emptiness, and exhaustion, and shows convincingly—the strength of the book lies here—how each one offers an opportunity for fuller growth. Turning the pages we maybe perceive how much of our life we fail to live, how many opportunities we waste. It is my hope that this book will reach a vast number of people experiencing the pain and splendor of being human. They will be enlightened and comforted."

—Ruth Burrows, OCD, author of *Essence of Prayer*

"In a nutshell, life is best defined as a conundrum. Every high flees the hot pursuit of a low; certainties emerge from the shadows of doubt; endings are invitations to new beginnings. In this beautiful book, Joan Chittister focuses her discerning eye upon these conundrums. Turning the pages is like turning a kaleidoscope of insight because it helps us to see, admire, and appreciate the infinite colors and shapes of life. At times, *Between the Dark and the Daylight* sparkles with ageless wisdom; at other times it glows like the quiet embers of a best friend's advice. This is a book to which you will return over and over, and, each time you do, you will discover new treasures of optimism."

—Maura Poston Zagrans, author of *Camerado, I Give You My Hand*

Between the Dark and the Daylight

Major Books by Joan Chittister

Called to Question: A Spiritual Memoir

The Fire in These Ashes:
A Spirituality of Contemporary Religious Life

Following the Path:
The Search for a Life of Passion, Purpose, and Joy

For Everything a Season

The Gift of Years: Growing Older Gracefully

Happiness

Heart of Flesh:
A Feminist Spirituality for Women and Men

Illuminated Life:
Monastic Wisdom for Seekers of Light

In Search of Belief

The Liturgical Year:
The Spiraling Adventure of the Spiritual Life

The Monastery of the Heart:
An Invitation to a Meaningful Life

A Passion for Life: Fragments of the Face of God

A Radical Christian Life:
A Year with Saint Benedict

Rule of Benedict: A Spirituality for the 21st Century

Scarred by Struggle, Transformed by Hope

Welcome to the Wisdom of the World:
And Its Meaning for You

Wisdom Distilled from the Daily:
Living the Rule of St. Benedict Today

BETWEEN THE DARK AND THE DAYLIGHT

EMBRACING THE CONTRADICTIONS OF LIFE

Joan Chittister

IMAGE
NEW YORK

Published in the United States by Image, an imprint of the Crown
Publishing Group, a division of Penguin Random House LLC, New York.

www.crownpublishing.com

IMAGE is a registered trademark and the "I" colophon
is a trademark of Penguin Random House LLC.

Library of Congress Cataloging-in-Publication Data
is available upon request.

ISBN 978-0-8041-4094-2
eBook ISBN 978-0-8041-4095-9

PRINTED IN THE UNITED STATES OF AMERICA

Book design by Anna Thompson
Jacket design by Kristen Vasgaard Ingebretson

10 9 8 7 6 5 4 3 2 1

First Edition

This book is dedicated to Susan Doubet, OSB,
because of whom so many of the paradoxes
of life become doable, are made livable, disappear.
She certainly makes my life easier.

Contents

Contents

THINKING THE UNTHINKABLE

There is a part of the soul that stirs at night, in the dark and soundless times of day, when our defenses are down and our daylight distractions no longer serve to protect us from ourselves. What we suppress in the light emerges clearly in the dusk. It's then, in the still of life, when we least expect it, that questions emerge from the damp murkiness of our inner underworld. Questions with ringtones that call the soul to alert but do not come with ready resolutions. Questions about life, not about the trivia of dailiness. The kind of questions to which there is no one answer but which, nevertheless, plague us for attention if we are ever to move through the dimness of life's twists and turns with confidence.

These questions do not call for the discovery of data; they call for the contemplation of possibility.

It is these kinds of questions that beleaguer the soul

from one end of life to the other. It is these questions that the great spiritual traditions of every age have always set out to face and tame.

But how does this happen and what does it demand of us if we are to brook the inexorable appearance of these confusions, these tormentors of the spirit, and bend them to the best in us?

The truth is that we spend our lives in the centrifuge of paradox. What seems certainly true on the one hand seems just as false on the other. Life is made up of incongruities: Life ends in death; what brings us joy will surely bring us an equal and equivalent amount of sorrow; perfection is a very imperfect concept; fidelities of every ilk promise support but also often end.

How can we account for these things? How can we deal with them? How can we find as much comfort in them as there is confusion? These are the queries that will not go away but which, the spiritual giants of every age knew, need to be faced if we are ever to rise above the agitation of them. There is a point in life when its paradoxes must be not only considered but laid to rest.

The great truth of early monastic spirituality, for instance, lies in the awareness that only when life is lived in the aura of the transcendent, in the discovery of the Spirit present to us in the commonplaces of life, where the paradoxes lie, can we possibly live life to its fullness, plumb life to its depths.

When seekers went out to the wasteland looking for spiritual direction from the Fathers and Mothers of the desert, they did not receive in response to their spiritual questions harsh exercises in self-denial. On the contrary.

They received instruction in self-knowledge. They received the wisdom of those who themselves had fathomed the tumult of life's paradoxes. They were instructed in the need to confront the tensions of them in their own lives. Not to deny them. Not to try to escape them. Not to ignore them. Not even to judge them. They were required to learn to see in the opposites of life the real richness of life.

Stories abound in the Christian tradition extolling the exploits of great spiritual figures whose fasts were Olympian, their years of solitude monumental, their rigorous disciplines on every level breathtaking. And so?

That kind of spiritual discipline is certainly impressive, but it does not represent the whole story. It is not even the greater part of the stories of any of the great spiritual eras or traditions. Seekers throughout the ages, the great mystics of every century, knew that it is not in physical asceticisms alone, let alone essentially, that the soul grows, expands, centers, and becomes its most radiant self.

In fact, the physical feats of those whose marks of the spiritual life lie in taxing the body and ignoring the world are, at best, more questionable disciplines to the age in which we live now than they are acceptable examples of an inspiring spiritual life. We flee them like the scourge. So what good were they?

If truth were known, that kind of spiritual heroism may well do more to discourage commitment to the spiritual life than to inspire it. So what is the stuff of the universal spiritual quest and path? What can possibly be found from across the ages as spiritual model for the likes of us?

To the average person whose life is exemplary most of all for its ordinariness—to people like you and me, for instance—it is what goes on inside of us that matters for the healthy life and real spirituality.

Clearly, the spiritual life begins within the heart of a person. And when the storms within recede, the world around us will still and stabilize as well. Or to put it another way, it was greed that broke Wall Street, not the lack of financial algorithms. Whatever it is that we harbor in the soul throughout the nights of our lives is what we will live out during the hours of the day.

This single-minded concentration on the essence and purpose of life, along with a focus on inner quietude and composure, makes for a life lived in white light and deep heat at the very core of the soul. Centering on the spirits within us, rather than being obsessed with the vicissitudes and petty imperfections of life gives the soul its stability, whatever the kinds or degrees of turbulence to be dealt with around it.

It is those elements of spirituality that this book is about, not extreme asceticisms or rejection of the world. Sometimes extolled in early spirituality, they are actually minor themes in the history of spirituality.

Nevertheless, this book has not been written for the sake of recording or repeating the wisdom of the past.

Instead, this book is meant to shine light on the inner confusions of our own age. It is written for all our sakes. For now—for this time and place, where we live our lives at the epicenter of chaos and crises from all directions. We are weary and worn out from its petty problems and daily stress, are in search of the quiet that calms confusion and clarifies insights and firms the path.

It is these paradoxes of our own times that skulk within us, that confuse us, sap our energy, and, in the end, tax our strength for the dailiness of life. They call us to the depth of ourselves. They require us to see Life behind life. Confronting the paradoxes of life around us and in us, contemplating the meaning of them for ourselves, eventually and finally, leads to our giving place to the work of the Spirit in our own lives.

And then will we have answers to it all? Probably not. Johann W. von Goethe wrote once, "Everything has been thought of before, but the problem is to think of it again." It is thinking through life alone, by ourselves or as communities of seekers with no particular or immediate instance in mind, that may save us from giving ourselves up to the enigmas of life in despair.

For all of us, paradox underlies the question of what it means to be human. These thoughts that rise out of nowhere in us between dark and dawn seem to have no content but will not let us rest. How is it that what is right at some times is not right at all times? What does it take to choose between them? This little book is an excursion into recognizing in the convolutions of this process the stuff of our own life of the spirit.

The Light Found in Darkness

Psychologists tell us that one of the most difficult conditions a person can be forced to bear is light deprivation. Darkness, in fact, is often used in military captivity or penal institutions to break down an individual's sense of self. Once a person becomes disoriented, once they lose a sense of where they are, and what it is that lurks in the dark around them, or where the next crevasse or wall or attack may be coming from—once they can no longer feel in control of their physical surroundings—a person loses a sense of self. Every shred of self-confidence shrivels. The giant within them falls and they become whimpering prey of the unknown. The natural instinct to be combative is paralyzed by fear. The spirit of resistance weakens. The prisoner becomes more pliable, more submissive, more willing to take directions.

It disarms a person, this fall into the sinkhole of sensory

deprivation. It can drive them to madness. It is, every military knows, an effective technique.

Nothing does more than darkness to isolate us from the sense of human support and understanding which, whether we're commonly conscious of it or not, is the human being's main source of self-definition. Indeed, darkness separates us from reality. It disorients a person both physically and psychologically.

Simple as it may seem, when the lights go out, we simply lose our bearings. The density of the dark makes it impossible for us to fix our positions anymore. We find ourselves alone in the universe, untethered and unprepared. The blackness of lightlessness leaves us no internal compass by which to trace or set our steps. Unlike the blind, few of us ever learn to develop our other senses enough to rely on them for information about the circumstances in which we find ourselves. Interestingly enough, it is those who consider themselves sighted who are most limited without light. And so, in the end, the tenebrous undermines the average person's self-confidence, affects their vision, leaves them totally vulnerable to the environment and out of touch with the people around them. And that is only its physical effects.

The darkness of the soul is no less spiritually punishing than is the loss of physical light to the psyche. We talk about faith but cannot really tolerate the thought of it. It's light we want, not shadow, certainty not questions. The aphotic, the place without images, is no less an attack on faith and hope than those periods in life when nighttime brings nothing but unclarity, nothing but fear. Where am I going? the soul wants to know. When will this be over? the mind wants to know. How can I get out of this sightless place I'm in? the heart demands.

The sense of being stranded in the midst of life, of having no way out of this smothering nothingness, this cul-de-sac of the soul, is enough to drain a person's very personality until there is little left to recognize. Where did the joy go all of a sudden? Where did the feeling of self-confidence disappear to in the midst of this emptiness? Just yesterday life was clear and vibrant. Today it is endlessly bleak. The darkness is unyielding. Nothing helps; nothing takes it away.

There is no light here, we think. But we think wrong.

There is a light in us that only darkness itself can illuminate. It is the glowing calm that comes over us when we finally surrender to the ultimate truth of creation: that there is a God and we are not it. Whatever we had assumed to be an immutable dimension of the human enterprise is not. In fact, it is gone and there is nothing we can do to bring it back. Then the clarity of it all is startling. Life is not about us; we are about the project of finding Life. At that moment, spiritual vision illuminates all the rest of life. And it is that light that shines in darkness.

Only the experience of our own darkness gives us the light we need to be of help to others whose journey into the dark spots of life is only just beginning. It's then that our own taste of darkness qualifies us to be an illuminating part of the human expedition. Without that, we are only words, only false witnesses to the truth of what it means to be pressed to the ground and rise again.

Darkness is a mentor of what it means to carry the light we ourselves have brought to blaze into the unknown parts of life so that others may also see and take hope. "Rabbi," the disciples begged of their dying master, "how can we possibly go on when you are gone?" And the rabbi answered them, "It is like this: Two men went into the forest together but only one carried a light. When they parted there, the one with the light went on ahead while the other floundered in the darkness." The disciples insisted, "Yes, that is how it is and that is why we are so frightened to be without you." The old man fixed them with a long, strong stare and said, "Exactly. That is why you must each carry your own light within you."

The light we gain in darkness is the awareness that, however bleak the place of darkness was for us, we did not die there. We know now that life begins again on the other side of the darkness. Another life. A new life. After the death, the loss, the rejection, the failure, life does go on. Differently, but on. Having been sunk into the cold night of black despair—and having survived it—we rise to new light, calm and clear and confident that what will be, will be enough for us.

Growth is the boundary between the darkness of unknowing and the light of new wisdom, new insight, new vision of who and what we ourselves have become. After darkness we are never the same again. We are only stronger, simpler, surer than ever before that there is nothing in life we cannot survive, because though life is bigger than we are, we are meant to grow to our fullest dimensions in it.

As Og Mandino says of it, "I will love the light for it

shows me the way, yet I will endure the darkness because it shows me the stars."

The stars that come with darkness are the new insights, the new directions, the new awareness of the rest of life that darkness brings. Then, at the end of the struggle with it, the spirit of resistance finally gives way to the spirit of life.

Then we are free to simply allow life to go on around us until the contours of it begin slowly to emerge out of the nothingness that our lives have now become. Then we know that a new day is on the brink, that new life is coming to us, that a new direction is finally coming clear again, that the light within us has come to spark.

2

THE DELUSION OF FRUSTRATION

The human soul, it appears, is an ageless thing. If we can believe the annals of spiritual seekers across time, whatever bothered it in the third century—anger, desire, jealousy, lust—is clearly still bothering it in the twenty-first. But now it has a twenty-first-century name to suit its style and validate its current claim to legitimacy. We call it the search for "peace of soul" and frame it as some kind of mystical prize.

In this case, the spiritual contest for peace of soul demonstrates itself in the propensity for frustration. It lies embedded in the human psyche, exuding annoyance, publicly prominent and quietly tyrannous at the same time.

Frustration whispers in the night of a kind of systemic discontent with our lives. Nothing is quite right, though, if we were forced to admit it, nothing is really wrong either. All we know is that we want something we're not getting.

The frustration of it all lies in the fact that we're sure we have a right to what we want. And we're also sure that we're not getting it because it's being obstructed by something, someone who has no right to deny us.

We talk about it freely and we court it consciously. We speak of not being able to finish our work because the noise in the office frustrates us. Or the speed of the computer frustrates us. Or children playing in the yard frustrate us. Or—my father's favorite—the sound of the vacuum cleaner at night frustrates us. A vacuum cleaner? A child? Office noises? A slow computer? Are these the things on which hang our lives' content? Hardly.

The glory of frustration, of course, lies in its propensity to justify our own responses to it which, in turn, frustrate the people around us.

The desert monastics in the third century spoke of the inner struggle that gives rise to such spiritual chafing. "Tell me what makes a monk," Macarius asks. And Abba Zacharias answers him, "As far as I can tell, I think anyone who controls himself and makes himself content with just what he needs and no more, is indeed a monk." Is indeed, in other words, one whose life centers on what counts rather than on the temporary irritations of it.

The lesson is clear. Learning to be contented with what we have—and no more—escapes us. The ancients tell us that, to develop spiritually, we must discover how to control ourselves in the face of what we claim to lack but have no right to expect.

Without it, frustration obstructs us from being what we are meant to be—loving parents, good friends, partners, holy participants in the creation of our worlds. Or, just as bad, it justifies our not doing what we are required to do—meeting our responsibilities, relating well to the people with whom we live life and doing the work the world needs to have us do. To claim to be frustrated in the midst of life's normalcies only defeats our desire to be a fully functioning human being. And, ironically, we do it to ourselves.

And why would that be? The case is clear. Frustration is something that does not exist—except within the self. It translates my world to me through the filter of my own need to control it. Frustration becomes the space we put between ourselves and the world around us. It forgives us the effort to live well in a world where noise is a given and the nature of computers is to crash. And so it becomes the dark cloud through which we see our world. Worse, frustration is the very thing that smothers our joy in it and blocks our growth, as well.

The truth is that frustration is not about options, as if we have the right to create an environment independent of the needs of those around us. The very notion of it is pure chimera, a fantasy. No, frustration is about something outside ourselves, outside our grasp, to which we make unwarranted claim.

Frustration is a cover-up for something we have yet to face in ourselves. It lies in what we decide we have the right to demand from life rather than in concern for what life demands of us.

But it keeps us awake at night. It troubles our souls fretting about tomorrow. We lose sleep arm wrestling in our hearts with those whose own lives keep prodding us beyond our willingness to go, to grow, to go on. And it is a delusion.

There is really no such thing as frustration, except in ourselves. We call frustrating anything we want the world to confirm as justification for being unable to control the way we think. It's what we use to explain the sour or pouty or demanding or manipulative attitudes we have developed. It is the right we assert to be less than we are capable of being.

The paradox of delusion is that, if anything, the very act of putting trivia between us and the world is exactly a sign that we need to question what it is that is undermining our ability to function well in normal circumstances. When we allow the inconsequential to affect our ability to really be consequential in life, the question must be faced: What is really bothering us?

Is it a matter of being unwilling to admit what underlies the impatience, the despair, the anger? Are we frustrated with the computer or with the fact that our need to get a new one has been consistently ignored? Are we frustrated with the children who are playing in the yard because we expect the world to give us perfect silence or because we are unaccepting of the family from which these children come? Are we annoyed with the person next to us at work for walking back and forth outside our door or because they have the position we would really like? What is it in us that the frustration signals but no one has helped us to identify?

Frustration and the simmering agitation that comes with it, invading our nights and annoying our sleep, is one of the dangerous spirits of the soul. It comes in the dark when we should be resting at peace with the world, in gratitude for the day, in hopes of an even more contented day tomorrow. To dispel it, we must begin to confront it in ourselves. It is time to identify the fires that drive our frustration if we are ever to come to know ourselves. It is time to decide whether such great unease is really worth our masking it in the paltry and the picayune.

Frustration is the signal that, indeed, something does need to change in our lives. But no one else can change it for us. Only we have the power to name it and to change it within ourselves.

Only then can we begin to rest in the arms of a God who stands by, ready to companion us through our confrontation with the self to the Spirit of Freedom that awaits us at the end of the journey to Truth.

Luigi Pirandello wrote of our capacity to fool ourselves: "'Truth' [is] what we think it is at any given moment of time." A better look may, then, find in us a greater truth—that if we give up clinging to control rather than to possibility— life is good, creative, welcoming, and here for us to taste in many flavors.

Then trivia becomes only trivia. We discover every day that there are greater things to concentrate on in life than the niggling, ordinary, commonplace little things we so often allow to fell us. The task of the truth teller is first to unmask the falsities that lie within ourselves so that the full range of life is now freed to be seen. Only then are we in a position to really examine what is worth getting frustrated about.

3

The Place of Tsunamis in the Ocean of Life

The waves rolling in from the Atlantic today were high and white and threatening. Then, later in the day, the ocean was suddenly very quiet again, very much itself and at peace with the world. I couldn't help thinking what a life lesson there is in that kind of undulation, in that kind of natural upset. Scientists call it the deposition of sand, gravel and sediment that comes from the recurring movement of the waves against a shoreline. It is storms, we see, that change and freshen and reshape the nature of the land.

It is a study in the movement of the human heart. No wonder we find it difficult to sleep at night as the ocean within us roars and rolls and carries us adrift from one place in life to another.

As I watched the waters crash against the headlands

and finally change from rough to smooth so clearly and so certainly, I realized that the whole scene encapsulates another one of the paradoxes of life. We spend our time intent on living constantly settled lives and call that peace. We are forever seeking peace and calm. At the same time, we forever forget—if we ever knew it—that peace is not a state of lifelessness. Life is not a lily pond; life is a bay inside an ocean. Peace is what comes to us after we negotiate the roiling, pounding waves of life lived one surge at a time.

When we roll and toss our way through a troubled sleep, it is so often about precisely that: how to meet the next wave crashing against our ordered, well-controlled lives. The question of why it is that nothing we do seems to enable us to get any kind of constant control over our lives rankles within us. We struggle against having to learn once more how to surf the features of the next phase of life and survive. We grasp for false calm at every turning of the day and call ourselves damned or cursed or burdened or beaten without it. And yet, if we were forced to live in the peace that is listlessness, we would die from the tedium of it all. We seduce ourselves into thinking that we like the lack of challenge. We forget how dull becalmed can be.

The strange thing is that we seldom stop to consider the value of the waves themselves.

The waves of life break into the center of our languor to remind us that the quality of our lives is not simply given to us, it needs to be earned. Life doesn't come cut to size; it requires shaping. Life is the way we deal with it as well as the way we look at it. The waves of life—those subtle but clear changes in old routines, or the established ambience, or social pattern, or daily practices—are designed to call our attention to the fact that underneath the apparently still waters around us, something is beginning to rumble and churn. Something is changing now. It is time to adjust, to cope, to grow again beyond our old stale selves. We cannot simply float through life forever.

Instead, every wave brings with it a new set of circumstances to consider. In our agitated sleep we know that we do not have the luxury of running away. We cannot, we know, simply ignore what's going on around us as if it were all someone else's problem. It will take its toll on us, we know. The shift in the neighborhood; the local election; the bank failures across the country; the growing violence in the streets; the derision of peoples unlike us; the suppression of women. It's not a matter of clinging to the past now. In fact, there is no past now; there is only a present in the process of convulsion. Of spiritual tsunami.

Those who insist on preserving yesterday when today has already swept it away like sand on a beach lose the opportunity to guide the present. Rather they insist on resisting the present to the point that it simply fails to notice them anymore. It is a choice whether to run the risk of becoming part of a comfortable but insignificant cult in a society that is passing or participate in the efforts of a society that is rushing to regain its balance in a headwind of major proportions.

It's important to remember in times of upheaval that high winds and great waves freshen life as well as threaten to swamp it. Everything new is not the end of the world.

Instead, it is the beginning of a new way of being alive that is based on the past but has already grown beyond it. It is too late now to stop the wave. It can only be absorbed and the beaches rebuilt to accommodate the changes.

Rogue waves are the dangerous ones; they are the ones that no one takes note of or prepares to manage. These are the movements we should have seen but did not. Or, worse, they are what we saw coming but refused to acknowledge in the hope that ignoring them would make them go away.

We do it in public life but we do it in our personal lives, as well. We deny the signs of a failing marriage, a job we don't really like anymore, the anger of the children, our own loss of interest in everything that had once been the very center of our lives.

We are masters of it in the public arena. We assume that we can keep whole portions of society muted in the system and pay no price for that. We are certain that an ocean or two can go on protecting us from the reality of globalization. We ignore the growing tensions. We begin to take polarization in our government, among our citizens, in our churches for granted while underneath it all, the components of inexpungible change build up, crying for attention, pressing toward fulfillment.

In fact, every great moment in history has meant a shift in the tectonic plates of the last, the one that sat motionless for too long. And down deep we know the truth of it: Our sands are shifting now and no amount of willing it were otherwise can possibly stop the process.

We struggle to maintain a dead past in the name of peace and refuse the new life that running water brings to everything. We confuse "stagnant" with "calm" and call it holiness. We miss the power of the paradox that peace is not passivity and that a living death is neither death nor life.

And all the while, we miss the new beaches that great waves bring from which to launch our new and vibrant lives.

The desire for a false peace may be the most powerful inner signal we have of our tendency toward a spiritual death wish. The historian Arnold Toynbee says of it, "The human race's prospects of survival were considerably better when we were defenseless against tigers than they are today when we have become defenseless against ourselves."

It is staying alive while we are alive that is the challenge. And it is only the ability to negotiate the waves of life that can possibly save us from choosing brackish water over a few tumbles in the churning—but renewing—whitecaps of time.

4

THE MIRAGE OF SECURITY

Security is a fragile thing. One day we have it; the next day we don't. The problem is, How is it possible to tell what is really security from insecurity?

The Sufis tell an ancient story that strikes at the heart of the issue of security, splits it open for all to see its fragility and makes us all think again about what it means to be secure.

Once upon a time, the old story reports, there was a bird that sheltered in the withered branches of an old tree that stood in the middle of a vast deserted plain. One day a whirlwind uprooted the tree. The bird was bereft. What would he ever do now? Where could he go? There were no other trees in sight. There were no berry bushes in this place. There were no companions with whom to flock for support. Alone and distraught, he flew and flew and flew hundreds of weary miles in search of sanctuary. Almost in despair and ready to give up, he suddenly saw it. There, over the last dune, was a forest of young trees. Each of them heavy with fruit. And thus began a whole new life.

The question with which the story leaves us but does not answer, however, is as important as the story itself: How long did this latest shelter last? In fact, what exactly is the life span of security? Of any security? And if we can't define the time span of the word security, why do we seek it with such passion?

The truth is that security is not so much a state of life as it is a state of mind. It is the eternal quest for safety, for knowing that the ground under us is firm and settled, for knowing that our life is still under our control. It's an important part of the human psyche, this assurance that life is predictable. It is only trust that enables us to roam through the world, one foot nailed to the ground, attached to the string that will lead us back to where we've come from. Just in case things go wrong out here we have somewhere to go back to again. Security in this sense is the lifeline that makes us free.

The problem is that what we call security, like any anchor, is also a mooring that ties people down. "Those who have cattle have care," the Kenyans say. The more we accrue— from money to jewelry to property to houses—the more we have to guard and tend and protect them. Until, pretty soon, we find ourselves spending our lives on taking care of everything our money has bought.

Security, at least in the form of money, is meant to provide us with options in difficult times and, of course, it does. But it does other things, as well, that too often become as much burden as blessing. Obsession with financial security can blind us to the joy of the present, for instance, or block us from daring a less financially attractive future.

There is a point at which security makes change difficult, if not impossible. It can take the spring out of life and put in its place nothing more than the memory of what it was to contemplate possibilities. How do we simply take off and hike across Europe or do youth camping in Colorado or water purification work in Africa and leave behind the works and accumulations of a lifetime? Instead, we find ourselves beholden to the successes and interests of the past—more caretaker than explorer now, more manager of the past than inventor of the future.

There is a fear factor in undue concern for security, as well. Rather than launch out to test and fulfill the rest of our abilities, we cling to the little we have. We take security at too great a price. We fail to move beyond what is safe, we abandon our dreams in favor of what is sure rather than strive for what is best for us.

Then, too late—if at all—we discover that the need for security begins to preclude all other thoughts. It is what plagues us at night and follows us during the day. We live full of worry that it might well disappear when we aren't looking. Security has done its worst: We are now prisoners of our own small designs. And the false freedom that was to have come with it is finally exposed for the hollowness of the promise it brings.

Worst of all, sooner or later we all discover the most egregious element of all about security: It is not only bogus, it is out of our hands. It is totally dependent on outside influences and circumstances over which we have no control, never did have any control, never will have any control. If you're Rockefeller, the stock market crashes; if you're on welfare, the government cuts the stipend; if you're Bernie Madoff, the police come.

And what, in the middle of the night, do you do then to assuage yourself of anxiety, to convince yourself to get up the next morning? There is only one way to deal with security: Don't worship it; don't count on it. But at the same time, understand that the universe is friendly. Something else is waiting for us over the next dune. As the ancients imply, for every dead and uprooted tree, there is another forest of young ones waiting to take us in.

Risk, the willingness to accept an unknown future with open hands and happy heart, is the key to the adventures of the soul. Risk stretches us to discover the rest of ourselves—our creativity, our self-sufficiency, our courage. Without risk we live in a small world of small dreams and lost possibilities.

Risk prods us on to become always the more of ourselves. It is the invitation to the casino of life.

Like the bird, we must be prepared at all times to move on, to keep trying, to realize that calamity is as much a part of life as security will ever be. And if security brings confidence as well as worry, calamity, as disruptive as it may be, will also bring us new growth and enlightenment.

5

THE INSECURITY OF CERTAINTY

So many of the illusions of life hide in full view. But we cling to them, nevertheless. We need them, perhaps, for reasons at first not apparent, even to ourselves.

Power, one of the major illusions of life, is the modern drug of choice. Its effects are everywhere to be seen. A trip to the pyramids in Egypt, for instance, promises a sure sign of it. Or if not there, a journey to Stonehenge in England, perhaps, or to Newgrange in Ireland ought to certify it for sure. All of these are monuments to ages long gone and societies forever disappeared. There are no tomes of history to explicate their glory. There are no steles or stone tablets or runes to cite their contributions to humankind. There are no relics of their triumphs or even of their losses.

There are no other clues to their existence. These powerful ones, certain of their security, came, they saw, they conquered, as the ancients put it—and then they disappeared.

There is nothing left by which to remember them, no great exploits to preserve, no moral achievements to emulate. Only one thing is clear. Their pyramids and markers and monuments have become memorials only to the deaths of the people who raised them in anonymity and left them in obscurity. The certainty of security—of power, of status, of money, of fame—of immutable claim to the good life, has escaped them all. However thick the walls they built around them, in the end they could not guarantee their own invulnerability. This kind of surety escapes all of us, as well.

The very thought of it—for workers, savers, strivers, winners all—haunts us. After all, why else work if not to achieve? We seek security like crabs in want of water. We expect our talents, triumphs, and proficiencies to be recognized, to be rewarded. We want our achievements noted, our status guaranteed. And we want more and more of both. We want everything we can have. We live with an open grasp outstretched. And at night, we fear the emptying of it.

The poet Percy Bysshe Shelley, also clearly plagued by the idea, wrote of it:

> *I met a traveler from an antique land*
> *Who said: "Two vast and trunkless legs of stone*
> *Stand in the desert. Near them on the sand,*
> *Half sunk, a shattered visage lies. . . .*
> *And on the pedestal these words appear:*
> *'My name is Ozymandias, King of Kings:*
> *Look on my works, ye mighty, and despair!'*

*Nothing beside remains. Round the decay
Of that colossal wreck, boundless and bare,
The lone and level sands stretch far away."*

This awareness of the transitoriness of life is deep in us, however stable life seems for us now. The question haunts us: Is this all there is?

The fear of loss, of change, of transition is the private nightmare of so many yet. We see houses, even of the wealthy, washed away in rogue storms. We watch bank accounts wither. We see food lines lengthen. We hear of businesses that have closed, of professionals who have been overwhelmed with debt, of last year's secure who have now become insecure. We fear, even in our security, the insecurity that stalks us all.

So we toss and turn at night. We stay awake trying to plan for the unexpected. But the very fact that a thing is unexpected makes planning a foolish and feeble exercise. Yes, he may die. Yes, the factory may close. Yes, the child may fail. Yes, the property values may decline and the medical bills go up. Yes, my kingdom, too, may disappear. The fear of it all clings to us in the darkness like the smell of damp in the woods.

Then, the next morning, however secure we are, we give even more energy to guaranteeing ourselves for life.

Certainty has its advantages, of course, seductive and sirenlike. It promises us immortal indemnity, yes, and it also brings with it the sweet taste of eternal delight. The problem is that its assertions are sterile, lifeless, frail. They bring no warranty of their warranty.

Certainty sits on the road in front of us and claims to make the angst of future planning unnecessary. After all, once I get what I want, I have it, don't I? But then why go on tossing and turning in the night unless, of course, I already know, down deep, that the real answer is, Who knows? Who knows when the sickness will come, when the institution will close? When the circumstances will change? Or worse, when I myself will tire of the routine of it? And wish for a wilder ride through life than certainty can ever give.

Certainty promises us a life free of care. And yet, even when we are most secure in our own definitions of eternal peace, of surety, of success, our expectations dull. After all, what else is there to want now? Life becomes routine, an exercise in a string of tomorrows just like our string of yesterdays.

But if we listen with a clearer ear to the voices of the soul when panic sets in, we may hear a different kind of message. We may come to understand that there are burdens that come with certainty as well as the promise of blessings.

It is possible, the heart tells us, that in our search for certainty we may be missing the graces that come with its attendant reality, fortuity.

The search for certainty always puts us in the position of having to foreclose on options that, however unsure or risk-laden, might even be better for us in the long run. Doing what we want to do rather than what we are sure can garner us a sure life in a sure place for a sure amount of time may actually be the more joyful, more fulfilling route for us. Then, we might be able to go to bed happy, alive with potentiality, rather than weighed down by the elusiveness of certainty.

When we opt for certainty, we make change inconceivable. When change comes unbidden and without our permission, it looks more dangerous than daring, more of an enemy than a liberator. The very intrusion of the unanticipated into our well-planned lives stands to shake life to its very foundations. Rather than simply invite us to move on to even more growthful pastures than the bogs into which we've settled, change that is unwanted, unexpected, unwelcomed threatens the very fiber of our lives.

Certainty, for all its guarantees, demands a subservient companion. It comes at the price of both liberty and creativity. It nails our feet to the floor and calls it success.

The wisdom of the night is a hard one to bear, perhaps, but the very matter of our discontent at the thought of change tells us that there are other lessons to learn in life. Mignon McLaughlin writes, "It's the most unhappy people who most fear change." We must come to understand that dullness is itself an irritant of the soul and it is the very uncertainty of certainty that prods us to grow.

It is the spirit of invention and possibility to which uncertainty calls us. What uncertainty brings us to is the security that comes with knowing that we finally developed in ourselves the ability to grow, to adjust, to become.

6

The Fragility of Achievement

There are ways of saying it on the streets that are less elegant than professionals might phrase it, perhaps, but it's difficult to say it better than the clichés: "What goes up must come down" is one kind of popular wisdom. Another says it a bit more subtly maybe but just as wisely: "Remember that the people you meet on the way up you'll meet again on the way down." The point is clear: Power and status are movable feasts. Nobody holds either of them forever or for sure. Negotiating between the two ends of the social scale is one of the major challenges of life, a mark of mental health and, in the long run, a measure of our happiness.

The social scale is a two-way street. The fact is that people go both up and down the social scale, inexorably, in every arena, always. These are the people who have become "famous" at whatever social level for some reason and then discovered the difficulty that fame brings.

Sometimes they're celebrities with unusual talent who outlived the talent that brought them to public attention and found themselves off the charts, off the stage, outside the social circle they had come to take for granted.

Sometimes they're politicians whose personal charisma swept them into public office but then suffered the disappointment of constituents whose expectations they could not meet.

Sometimes they're just people like you and I who were local company CEOs and had a change of personal fortune. In many cases they were trusted businesspeople who steered a local company into bankruptcy. Often they are anyone who has achieved some kind of public recognition or responsibility and then wakes up one morning to find out that the committee has been disbanded or the office has been eliminated or simply that the people who once asked you for answers to their questions are now calling somebody else.

More commonly than we realize, they're average middle-aged couples once identified by the local church as "Family of the Year" who then had to bear the headlines in the local paper trumpeting the fact that their child had been convicted for dealing drugs. Whatever the situation, the sun has shifted in another direction, the star over my life has faded, one of my reasons for getting up in the morning has gone.

The truth is that all social positions, no matter how small or how large on anybody's sociometric scale, are fragile. They depend in some instances on term lengths alone: After so many years in an office no matter how much a person likes a position, fits the position, it ends. The psychological impact of being removed from something simply because the time is up, whether the person's interest or capacity for the work is up or not, is necessarily unsettling.

In other situations, because membership itself changes, because the needs of the time change, too, as the years go by, the expectations of the members change, as well. Then it's not too long before the officeholders themselves begin to feel distance grow up between them and the very people who once cheered them there. Sometimes it's as simple as seeing the work of a lamplighter consumed by the new electric switch, of seeing the artistry of my life, the talent for which I have been acclaimed, replaced by the new technology.

Even celebrities know the pressure of having public tastes change toward them, however talented they may be.

In every instance, support flags, energy fades, endurance pales.

Whatever the particular situation that prompts a major life change for those who have known the exhilaration of public approval, however limited and local, or the abrupt loss of the public spotlight, as well, the moment is a major one, can even be traumatic for some. Of all the things in a person's life that require a person to literally begin again, this may be the most impacting. This one is not simply a time of progressive change from one level of involvement to another in the same area. This one involves a real reappraisal of the self. And often a sense of loss, of no place to go, of having life stopped in midflight.

And so, in the light of such fragility, how do people

whose lives depend on this kind of public function sleep through the night with time nipping at their heels, bringing them closer by the day to the end they know must come but do not want? What is the answer then to the question, Where do I go now? What do I do now? What is my life about now?

The fact is that the preparation for a change of status, any status, must begin even before the change occurs. Years before life becomes consumed by the public and its public functions, the healthy person decides never to be held captive to the masks of officialdom. Never to become the role in which they find themselves. Never to surrender a private life to a public one.

It is a matter of making sure that a single dimension of life does not consume all the other ones—family, friends, personal interests and basic and fundamental human goals. It is, as young people argue, a matter of "getting a life" that is not consumed by a role, by a position, by a function that will just as easily become someone else's position tomorrow as my own today.

Few American presidents managed to stay as close to people and real life as Harry Truman did. Every day he simply got up and walked around the block, meeting new friends, greeting old ones, becoming part of the environment. As a result, when his term of office was over, there was no neighborhood to go back to because he had never left it.

Keeping up with old hobbies or developing new ones protects us from becoming one-dimensional people in one-dimensional positions.

Creating other equally avid interests—like research or academics or philanthropy as Condoleezza Rice or Jeb Bush or Jimmy Carter did—provides another world equally important, equally impacting to go to when the first one ends. More important, it gives us an even broader definition of ourselves than any single position can ever provide.

Then life becomes an ongoing drama made up of many chapters, not a one-act play that leaves us all dressed up with no place to go when that act ends. Then life is rich and full and exciting and real all the way to the grave.

It is easy in a world of plastic celebrities, people whose lives are made on Madison Avenue by photographers and advertising moguls, to confuse the nature of a position with what it means to be a person. In this country, we are all defined by what we do—Kelly Somebody, high school English teacher—rather than by what we are: kind, just, honest, hardworking. What we *are* is reserved for our obituary, what we *do* determines the way we're identified now. Such a pity. It means that one part of us has consumed the rest of us—to the point where, far too often, we ourselves confuse the two and lose sight of the dimensions of our lives that really count.

Dag Hammarskjöld, past secretary-general of the United Nations, writes of our real purpose as real people, a criterion that goes beyond anybody's role description. He says, "You have not done enough, you have never done enough, so long as it is still possible that you have something to contribute."

It's those qualities that in the end define us and that never end with the term.

7

THE EMPTINESS OF ACCUMULATION

In a capitalist society consumption is a national virtue. It is its backbone, its engine, the mainframe at the very center of the society. We measure our society's well-being by keeping precise records of the amount of consumption we do. We use percentages to signal how much better or worse we were at buying things this year than we were last. We celebrate our gross national product when we never even consider calculating our gross national distribution of goods, and we define buying as a sign of national health. It's buying, after all, that sustains the economy. And sustaining the economy is what a capitalist system is all about. "The chief business of the American people," President Calvin Coolidge said, "is business."

At the height of the worst national tragedy in U.S. history, the 9/11 terrorist attacks in 2001, President Bush ended his first television message to the American public by telling them that the most important thing they could do in the face of such a devastating attack was to "keep our economy going . . . to go shopping more." The whole world must have drawn breath on that one.

In the face of the first foreign attack on U.S. soil since the War of 1812, in the middle of the smoking rubble that carried the ashes of over three thousand civilians, there was something about the message that rang hollow, that broke the heart, that lacked soul. No talk of discovering reasons for such an attack. No talk of reaching out to allies in the Middle East. No talk of bringing the height of U.S. justice to this devastating situation. No talk about being our spiritual best at such a time as this. No, the god who would save us from this disaster, Bush was clear, was the god of the free market.

And yet, why wouldn't we be a society of consumers? What other basic value do we learn in a world where developing excess want is more important than meeting basic needs? In societies such as these the people who manage to accumulate the most things are considered the most successful. So we sell and we buy and we buy and we sell, all of us trying to catch up and keep up and get more tomorrow than we had yesterday. We live in a whirlwind of exchange where we market to three-year-olds on the television sets in their playrooms and begrudge retirement monies to those who spent their whole lives making the very things we want everybody else to buy.

The problem, of course, is that the never-ending marathon of marketing that is required to maintain such a system is now sucking the rest of the world into it, as well.

Poor societies, which cannot afford the goods we buy, make the goods wealthy societies consume at lesser pay and great cost to the quality of their own lives.

At the same time, the quality of our own lives, drowned in adult toys and public playthings, are just as surely being smothered by them, too.

Judging from the front page of every newspaper we print, every television program we watch, every deteriorating school and bombed-out neighborhood and pitted road and overloaded electrical grid and homeless family in the nation—in a nation awash in the flotsam and jetsam of things—there's something missing that is far more important than the gadgets we have chosen in its stead. We are bartering our souls for the sake of what will be tomorrow's refuse.

In every great spiritual tradition, in most modern measures of psychological health, the tendency to excessive consumption is seen as a sign of deep personal need, the kind no amount of artifacts can supply. Then, it isn't what we have that marks us; it's what we don't have and are trying to substitute for them that signals danger.

It's a sense of great cloying want that dogs us through our days and haunts our nights which, in the end, corrupts our hearts and sours whatever joy today's accumulation masks. We get addicted to things as surely as some people get addicted to alcohol or drugs. They are our signs to ourselves that we are really worth something. And yet, ironically, it is precisely what we lack that they signal most.

Sometimes it's status we're looking for in buying the bigger house, the extra cars, the larger piece of property. Things that will put us into debt and under pressure for years while we look for social approval or public respect. And all the while, if truth were told, it's the people who scrubbed every table and took down the booths after every civic holiday that people remember. It's only righteousness and character that bring a person lasting honor.

Often it's love we're looking for, only to discover that things can buy us sycophants but never affection or concern. Those things come from being lovable, not from being ostentatious.

Commonly, we invest in things as trappings, as signals, as badges of success when we lack the confidence to believe in our self. As Anna Quindlen says of it, "There was a period when I believed stuff meant something. I thought that if you had matching side chairs and a sofa that harmonized and some beautiful lamps to light them you would have a home, that elegance signaled happiness."

The price we pay for the accumulation of things is a high one. For the rest of our lives we are condemned to fear the loss of them and to live forever with the taste of continual insecurity in our mouths, unending neediness in our hearts and the inability of soul to enjoy what we have and be grateful for what we love.

The things of the soul—the joy of life, the love of beauty, the gift of friendship, the integration into nature, the pursuit of truth and the depth of the spirit—grow in open land, bare of the baubles of life, free of frenzy and devoid of the chaos of accumulation. Then we are rich. Then we are strong. Then no one can take anything away from us because we have already relinquished it. Or, as the philosopher Epictetus wrote: "Wealth consists not in having great possessions, but in having few wants."

8

THE POVERTY OF PLENTY

There are two kinds of people in the world, we're fond of saying on St. Patrick's Day. And it's true. The only problem is that we confuse the categories.

The first kind is the politician who was asked in the course of a recent election, as a matter of economic comparison, how many houses he owned. The candidate struggled for an answer. "Well, I'm not sure right now," he said slowly, trying hard to remember, "six or seven, I guess."

The second kind is the homeless street beggar who found a diamond and platinum engagement ring in his begging bowl and, instead of pawning it, put it aside for safekeeping until the stranger who had dropped it there by accident returned three days later to look for it.

Both types of people are poor. But only one of them knows it. And that in itself is another kind of poverty.

The poverty of plenty is a state of mind where enough

is never enough. It is an agonizing situation to be in, this spider's web of unending desire. The psychoanalyst Erich Fromm said of it, "Greed is a bottomless pit which exhausts the person in an endless effort to satisfy the need without ever reaching satisfaction."

Greed, in other words, is the engorgement of the soul, a spiritual obesity that consumes one bite of life after another without ever bothering to really taste the prize. For these people, life is not about enjoying things, it is simply about having them. It is about collecting the trophies of life, like hunters who hang moose racks in their living rooms long after the hunt is over.

In a life like this, everything grows redundant, nothing more than an upgrade of last year's model. Extra cars sit in the garage undriven. The houses are never lived in. The expensive watches are in a display case. And the poverty of soul, like a cancer cell, begins to eat away at the rest of life.

The even more interesting dimension of the dilemma is that the syndrome does not simply attach itself to wealth. Very economically average people who allow things to define them can be just as drugged by the desire to possess, rather than driven by the need to become even more of a human being than they already are. The point is that we can all become glutted by the pursuit of things rather than the pursuit of life.

To be satiated, glutted, is to lose the sense of taste for life. There is no enjoyment anymore. The definition of life becomes "Been there, done that." So what is left to hope for, or what remains to be seen, and which of life's mountains is yet to be climbed?

Hoarding becomes the taste that poisons every other taste in life until finally we pile up so many things we no longer remember or really feel the thrill of having them. With the sense of newness goes the grace of appreciation, one of the more important dimensions of life. The ability to appreciate the delights of life and the gifts of people and the thrill of unfamiliar events, rather than simply taking them for granted, is what gives tomorrow special meaning. One brand-new fishing pole is a luxury; seventy-two of them is nothing more than a muddle of fishing rods. As Dryden said, "Plenty makes us poor." Bereft of the power of the singular experiences of life, like children with too many toys, we don't know which one to play with next. So we simply sit and look at them. And for what purpose?

Appreciation is the grace of sensibility, of really experiencing every moment for its uniqueness and its awe. It is what enables a person to stand on a street corner, arms out wide, head up, smiling the smile of the holy and giving thanks for the depth of every moment of it. It is the posture of the heart that says life is good, I am blessed, the universe is friendly, the world is beautiful. As Julian of Norwich said, "In this acorn is everything that is." The one who has learned to appreciate says, "In this moment is the essence of everything glorious I have been given in life—and it is enough."

But to those who have not learned the piercing power of appreciation, the taste buds of life grow dull.

To have everything is to have nothing. Overwhelmed by quantity we lose all awareness of life crystallized into small pieces of joy and insight and gratitude. It is the death of the soul.

The fine art of having something left in life to want gives people the power of purpose. Something to strive for stretches us. Something to work for teaches us things we would never have tried to learn any other way. Something to be grateful for enables us to know the power of gratuitous love, the willingness of others to sacrifice themselves for us without any thought of reward for having done it.

Instead, the poverty of plenty costs us the headiness of delight. It deprives us of the intoxication of small joys. It leaves us with little to look forward to, with nothing to reach for, with the cold hard reality of having nothing new in life to wait for in the long cold days of winter.

"Keeping up with the Joneses," of all possible reasons for drowning the soul in a plethora of things, has got to be one of the world's puniest guides through life. Surely the purpose of life has got to be about something greater than competing with neighbors who don't even know they're in a contest.

"Poverty of goods," Montaigne wrote, "is easily cured; poverty of soul, impossible." I'm not quite so pessimistic about poverty of soul as Montaigne is. I think that engorgement with goods, like any other unbalanced diet of bananas or chocolate or ice cream or steak, soon becomes unpalatable, sickening, inedible, noxious. Sooner or later, in desperation perhaps, people will be forced to go inside themselves to find the parts of life and soul that are not being nourished and figure out why. Then, surely, they will stop to enjoy what they have and detach themselves from the glitter to find the glory of life.

There is really only one small difference between the politician who had so many houses that he couldn't remember exactly how many and the homeless man who had nothing and yet gave the diamond ring back to the woman who had accidentally left it in his cup: One of them had everything and was satisfied with nothing; the other had nothing and was satisfied.

And there is a cure. The Chinese philosopher puts it very succinctly, "Manifest plainness, embrace simplicity, reduce selfishness, have few desires." Once we do that, we will all rest better at night.

9

The Role of Failure in Success

For some, the greatest fear of them all is the fear they feel for the coming day. For the meeting tomorrow. For the report tomorrow. For the speech tomorrow. For the test tomorrow. For the game tomorrow. What if I fail? And we say the unspoken always, What will I lose as a result? It's a pity. The question ought to be, And if I fail tomorrow, what will I gain as a result?

Don't be mistaken: Failure is not a prescription for the good life, but failure is indeed inevitable. It's not a terminal disease. If anything, it may have a great deal more to do with a healthy mental attitude toward life than success can ever breed.

In an earlier period, adults liked to see children play sports because, they said, they wanted their children to learn to lose. Not now. Now, the hype is so high, the adult investment in children's games so serious, the public attention so intense that the stress of it, the fear of failure, now follows children from Little League at the age of six through all their born days.

When they could be learning the lifelong lessons of failure, they are now practicing to throw a ball higher, faster, farther, with more accuracy than some little six-year-old neighbor. Until eventually throwing the ball becomes more important than running in the field or playing with other children or learning to laugh at themselves when they fall short of the goal and flat in the mud at the same time.

The problem is that the lessons we do not really intend to teach them—practice, practice, practice, prevail, win at all costs—are too often precisely the ones they learn. And those lessons, learned in childhood, can affect us for life, years after the game playing is over and the stakes are real this time.

One thing for sure: No one escapes failure. The bad business deal happens, the promotion goes to someone less experienced, the crop dies, the Christmas tree falls over on Christmas morning, all the ornaments broken with the in-laws coming at noon for the perfect dinner. We don't win and we break down. No doubt about it: Success can be every bit as demanding as failure.

We find ourselves in a situation where winning all the time is at least as bad as failing. "The toughest thing about success," Irving Berlin, the great composer, wrote, "is that you have to go on being a success."

We all have within us the scars that come from failing to lose once in a while. "The smell of the greasepaint, the roar of the crowd," circus performers call it as they go back again and again into the lion's cage, to the top of the trapeze to risk their lives for the approval, the applause, the social status that comes with winning. Who wouldn't fear losing once they have learned that to be acceptable to others you must always win?

The irony of it all is that it is only failure that inures us to losing. We need failure to learn that we don't need to win to justify the reason for our existence. Winning is part of life, yes, but human beings can live healthy, happy lives without it.

We are not born to win; we are born to grow, to develop, to become the best of ourselves—and to enjoy life. We're not here to turn life into a trophy machine. Somewhere along the line, we learn that second place is not good enough. Athletes lose silver medals in milliseconds in the Olympics and consider themselves losers. As some apocryphal philosopher taught, "No one ever remembers who came in second." Well, maybe not, but few people ever remember who came in first either.

No, life is not about winning. It is about trying, about participating, about striving, about becoming the best we can be, not the best by someone else's measure. That's what failure does for us. It teaches us about ourselves: our energy level, our endurance level, what we're naturally good at and what we're not, what we like and what we don't, what it means to do something just for the fun of it. Failure doesn't mean that we cannot compete; it doesn't mean not to give everything we have to doing what we do. It does mean that just because we play we don't have to win. The playing is the thing.

Most of all, it gives us the permission to go through life without public certification. Failure enables us to take risks as we grow until we find where we really fit, where we can not only succeed, but also enjoy the challenges of life as well.

No, winning is not everything. But we will never really know that until we lose a few and discover that the world does not end when we lose. Now it is just a matter of trying again somewhere else, perhaps. Now we're free to be unnoticed. We're free to do what we like best, what is needed most, what will bring us to the most we can be: the most happy, the most competent, the most satisfied with who we are and what we do. That means, of course, that we have to make choices about what we want to do and why we want to do it.

It's not easy to establish priorities in life. Most of life is spent needing to do everything at once. And that's impossible. At least it is impossible to do them all at the same level of artistry all the time. There are simply some things worth doing that at some times are worth doing poorly. Sometimes the soufflé doesn't come out as raised as we would like it, but it is food on the table and that is all that matters for now.

The ability to deal with failure, with doing some things well enough without having to do them compulsively, is a great gift.

One of life's greatest failure stories is about Manteo Mitchell, leadoff runner on the USA's 4x400 relay team for the 2012 Olympics. The United States had won every Olympic gold medal in the 4x400 relay race since 1980.

This year's competition from the Bahamas was good but Team USA had the edge. Manteo Mitchell set up for the first leg of the qualifying round, relieved to know that, despite the fact that his leg felt sore from a fall he suffered his first day in the Olympic Village, he was full of energy and ready to go. But then, suddenly, in the middle of the race with 200 meters to go, he felt his leg snap. "I let out a cry," he said later, "but with all the noise no one heard me." And then with one last great effort, he kept on running on a broken leg and enabled the team to qualify for the finals. "I knew something happened but I didn't want to quit and let the rest of the guys down," he said.

Team USA did not win the relay in the 2012 Olympics without him, but Manteo Mitchell showed the world that it's not winning that really defines a person. It's seeing your responsibilities through to the end, it's finishing what we start that counts. But Manteo warns us, as well, that fear of failure may itself be destructive. To do what we do to our utmost is one thing; to go beyond what is truly developmental simply for the sake of winning is another. The ability to tell one from the other is of the essence of psychological adulthood.

Then, whatever happens, we have developed into full and happy human beings. Failure, we come to understand, is what, in the end, makes a real success of us all. Logan Piersall Smith, whom few recognize or remember, for obvious reasons, may understand the whole paradox best. He writes: "How can they say my life isn't a success? Have I not for more than sixty years got enough to eat and escaped being eaten?" Or to put it another way, who's to say that just because Cornelius Vanderbilt made millions selling railroad cars doesn't mean that the rest of us can't be just as happy with life by being able simply to pay our bills. It all depends on our definition of success.

10

The Success of Failure

I heard a professor of communications tell a story once that completely changed the way I looked at the relationship between success and failure. A young boy, he related, received a dartboard for Christmas and immediately began to play with it. The first dart he threw hit the bull's-eye! Excited, the father called the child's mother into the room. The second dart the boy threw hit the bull's-eye again! Wide-eyed with pride, the father gathered the entire family. The third dart the boy threw was another bull's-eye! Then the boy stopped throwing darts and put the dartboard away. No amount of coaxing could get him to open the game again.

In this society, winning has always been everything. It's in our national DNA. We claimed a continent by subduing the people who were already here. We made ourselves a nation by waging wars that were either so small our adversaries don't even remember fighting them or so large that our adversaries' greatest mistake was to discount us. But win we did. And, in the end, it was out of that national myth that we spun a national self-image that colors our thinking to this day.

In this country to be number two at anything rather than number one—to be .001 of a second behind the leader, to take the silver medal rather than gold in anything—is to fail. "Nobody remembers who was number two," adults tell children, and so mark generations of winners with the scars of hidden shame where the feeling of success should be.

But that perspective on life is itself a sad commentary on what it says about a person who has the will to try. As a result, failure gets short shrift here. And that's the shame of it. The child with the dartboard knew what his father did not intuit: A record like his could only be shattered, not enhanced. From now on he could only be known for losing because he could never win so much again. It is an awareness long cultivated in a society that starts distributing trophies and blue ribbons to three-year-olds.

We fear the public humiliation of not being first. We shrink from being willing to try and so we never learn that achievement is not a public thing. Achievement is the awareness within us that we have stretched ourselves to the full length of ourselves. We have become the best we know how to be. And it is failure that teaches us that. Failure, in fact, is a necessary part of the process of real and ultimate success.

As a result, whole generations grow up never appreciating that simply being willing to compete at anything is worth the effort. To participate in anything that does not guarantee that I will be chosen is an act of great humility. It means that we are willing to put ourselves in the public arena and trust our dignity and efforts to the responses of the crowd. It is a cry for public support and respect. To make only winning worthy of respect is to demean everyone else in the process, to debase all the others who clearly have an ability and risk the response of the crowd.

But failure is about more than competitive events; it's about deep commitment to personal development. It asks of us a searing question: If I am not willing to fail, why not?

Failure is a teacher. Without failure we can only guess at what success could really look like if we exercised ourselves just a little bit more, practiced more often, tried more earnestly. Trial and error is not loss. It is the stepping-stone to success. Without failure all we have is untried ability. Accent on "untried."

When we set out with all our hearts to star in any given domain of life and do not, we have not failed. At most, we have discovered that our gifts are elsewhere, that happiness for us is a matter of being able to give some other gift. Untold numbers of people have learned by being refused a degree in, say, computer programming that their true calling is working with the disabled, or becoming a teacher, or doing interior decorating or selling real estate or doing anything on the planet except computer programming. In failure, they have learned to be grateful by having tried and failed.

When what I do makes me feel more inferior than

happy, more a failure than a success, more embarrassed than confident, failure gives me the chance to reassess my course in life. We are not born to be miserable. We are born to be fully alive, to be happy, to give our gifts to the world with the joy that comes from doing our best and having it mean something to someone else.

Failure gives us the chance to experiment with life, to play with it a bit, to move in different directions until we find, as we learned from Cinderella as children, the shoe that fits. Because what doesn't fit will irritate us all our life. We will live in the unnecessary pain that comes from forcing ourselves into something that not only embarrasses us but cramps our hearts and damps our spirits.

Life is about participating in the fine art of finding ourselves—our talents, our confidence, our sense of self, our purpose in life. The world waits for each of us to give back to the best of our ability what we have been given for its sake. The only way to know what that is depends on learning to follow our hearts until our hearts and our abilities are one, until what we love and what we do well are one and the same thing.

That is the prescription that leads always and forever to happiness. What greater success can there possibly be?

"Success," Ben Sweetland points out, "is a journey, not a destination." The very act of exploring possibilities in life is one more step up the ladder of success. What we reject—or what rejects us—along the way has a great deal to tell *us* about life, about happiness, about ourselves. It is the soul's search for what it means to come home to the self.

About life we learn that it is not fair—if my definition

of *fair* is that I will get what I want as I go. No, some of what I want either I cannot do or it is simply not available to me. Surprise.

About happiness I learn that I can get a lot of what I want that does not really fit me no matter how much I want it and that it will make me miserable in the end.

About myself I learn that whenever I do well what I am capable of doing, it doesn't make a bit of difference if it is perceived as a plum position or not: I will be outrageously happy doing it.

O. A. Battista unmasks the real from the unreal in life. He tells us, "You have reached the pinnacle of success as soon as you become uninterested in money, compliments or publicity." Then, as long as you are doing what you like doing best, there is really no way you can fail.

11

The Energy That Comes from Exhaustion

"I've got a great ambition," Thomas Carlyle wrote. "[It is] to die of exhaustion rather than of boredom." It's a lofty aim, of course, but it is important to remember that both dimensions of life—both ambition and boredom—threaten the quality of life. One by stretching a person beyond the limits of physical or mental endurance, the other by allowing the life that's in us to stagnate, to languish, to waste away. The effects of both are equally pathological: Exhaustion drains us physically; boredom depletes the soul.

But the situation is even more complex than that.

Medicine warns about the effects of exhaustion, yes, but carefully so. Stress upon stress—unending stress—they tell us, can wear the human system to a frazzle, to the point where one organ after another collapses under the wear of it. At the same time, they tell us in the next sentence, it is also true that good stress, stress that brings the system to its highest pitch—the heart pounding, the lungs full, the legs going at full bore—aerates the entire system, stretches it to its fullest, gives us life.

On the other hand, boredom smothers the heart to death and leaves us staring into space without a song to sing, a road to travel, or a reason to get up in the morning.

So, a person can die either way: by wearing down or by withering. Choose.

Me, I choose exhaustion. I'm with the better-to-burn-out-than-to-rust-out crowd. At least today. The question, of course, is, Why choose to extend the self rather than to save the self? And which is really which? And how does one choose between the two anyway when the night thoughts pull us this way and that: "I should quit; I must go on; I need to stop; I have so much to do yet. It's all for nothing anyway. An inch at a time it's changing." Toss this way; roll that way. Which will it be?

The direction we choose lies in the tendency of the soul toward its own growth. If enough is enough for me, then I will settle down and wait for life to come to me. If it does. On the other hand, if no amount of life satisfies me unless it is all the life I can come by, then I will reach out running and grasp for it. I will spend every bit of energy I have in its service. It's a matter of choosing to sit and watch the carousel of life go round or deciding to get up and ride it.

When the athlete steps over the finish line, bends halfway to the ground, breathing hard and gasping for more, it is years of practice and self-denial and commitment that crosses that line. It is years of the kind of unremitting, austere discipline that would make a monk cringe in shame. And it doesn't really matter whether the athlete wins the race or not. The fact is simply that they ran it. They spent their entire lives preparing for these three minutes, for the right to be among the runners of life, with all their hearts.

But what can we possibly get from such toil, such drudge, such grind that makes that kind of exertion and sacrifice and pain worthwhile? The answer is an easy one. We get the joy of achievement. To drive ourselves to our best in any arena—intellectual, physical, spiritual—is to know outside boundaries we never knew we had. At the same time, it taps into inner depths we never dreamed were there. It requires of us just one more stride, one more deep breath, one more final effort over and over and over again. And we give the most of ourselves because we have spent years storing it up to give.

It is a simple answer but it is the only one that comes back to us from the mirror. It is the effort that drops us tired on the field of life but feeling good about the exhaustion. It is the sheer joy of knowing that we gave back to life everything we were given when we came into it. It is the stamp of authenticity. It is spiritual fair trade.

Exhaustion tells us how really far we can go. It gives us a measure of ourselves that is realistic rather than fictional, honest rather than imaginary. It strips us of any false pretenses. We don't lie awake at night, then, telling ourselves that we could do it if we wanted to do it, if we did a little more of this, a little less of that. No, exhaustion tells us exactly what we are capable of doing rather than fooling us into thinking that we are something we are not. Exhaustion keeps us honest about ourselves.

There is a feeling of readiness for life that comes with having exhausted ourselves for something worthwhile. We know now that we are prepared for the next race life has to offer us. We know now that we can endure. Perhaps, even prevail. It is enough to enable us to bear every small burden so that when the great burdens come we will be there to carry our load.

The dull life, on the other hand, is a calm life, yes, and the bland life can claim a kind of unplumbed if not placid peace. But the purposeless life—life without passion, without commitment, without the investment of the whole self—is a vacuous life seeking a credible reason to bring energy to anything. More important, to be dull is not necessarily stressless, remember. "There is no fatigue so wearisome," Charles Haddon Spurgeon writes, "as that which comes from lack of work." The stress of stresslessness undoes the soul before it depletes the body.

The important choice in life, then, is to choose our stresses carefully. The good ones enliven us and give life to those around us. The bad ones give nothing to anyone, ourselves least of all.

One tastes life and finds it energizing; the other stares into space, vapid and empty of light. One shapes faces of stone and puts light in people's eyes. The other raises lassitude to an art form. One rolls and tosses at night excited by the thought of tomorrow's challenges. The other rolls and tosses with dread for the coming of one more barren day.

No doubt about it: There is an energy in the exhaustion that comes from meeting life head-on, a signal to the world that we are here, a sign to ourselves that life for us has been everything it is meant to be.

12

The Productivity of Rest and Recreation

The nice thing about the human body is that it wears out. It wears down. It can, as the Rule of Benedict says in chapter 64, be "overdriven." To be more precise, the Rule is talking about the abbot or prioress in the chapter when it says, "They must so arrange everything that the strong have something to yearn for and the weak nothing to run from."

The point is clear: Good leadership does not ask more of the worker than the worker is capable of doing. Whatever happened to that kind of wisdom? And how much further can we possibly go unless we rediscover the value of such an insight?

The really interesting aspect of such an ancient directive is that it was written in the sixth century, before light-bulbs, before humanity could do little or anything about extending the day into the night and veritably erasing the difference between the two. In those days, when the sun went down, people went to bed. "Make hay while the sun shines," the farmers said—and for good reason—since there was surely no way to make it otherwise. Days were measured from sunup to sundown. They were not divided into shifts. Darkness covered the earth and with it came silence, and rest, and recuperation time in preparation for the day to come.

It was a far cry from a world in which the Internet links the ends of the earth twenty-four hours a day. Before the Industrial Revolution engines did not continue to pound out bottle caps long after most workers went home for supper. Trucks did not race on in a mad dash to link the world's cities so that packages of widgets would be delivered in twenty-four hours and modernity could triumph. The writing did not go on late into the night. The offices did not stay open. The problem solving did not continue. The schoolwork did not begin after the parties ended. Yesterday's work did not get done in the middle of the night so that tomorrow's work could start again in five more hours.

And human beings were not taking sedatives to cope with stress or drugs to calm down. The medical community was not warning people about the effects of sleep deprivation. And surgeons were not beginning another operation at the end of an eighteen-hour day.

We drive ourselves relentlessly from one exhaustion to another. We pace our societies by the pace of our computers. We conduct the major relationships of our lives—both professional and personal—according to the speed of our communications. We measure ourselves by the amount of our productivity and every day we become more exhausted, less rested in body, spirit and mind, and so less capable of producing things, let alone of developing relationships, as a result. That's not irony, that's tragedy. And though we know it, we do not know what to do about it.

Now the question is a simple one: Are the ancient insights only that: ancient? Or are they wisdom because they have been carried down to every generation and found to be true?

Well, no less a person than Thomas Aquinas, easily considered the most brilliant man of the thirteenth century and a good candidate for every century after that, said about rest and recreation: "It is requisite for the relaxation of the mind that we make use, from time to time, of playful deeds and jokes."

And in the sixteenth century, Leonardo da Vinci, one of the most prolific geniuses of all time, wrote: "Every now and then go away, have a little relaxation, for when you come back to your work your judgment will be surer. Go some distance away because then the work appears smaller and more of it can be taken in at a glance and a lack of harmony and proportion is more readily seen."

Point: The grind is destructive of both the person and the work. Unless the soul can be refreshed enough to think, to create, to recoup both its energy and its interest in the work at hand, there is no hope for either recall or creativity.

Every year surveys report the decline of U.S. excellence in one arena after another. Even our children—the hard workers, the ambitious, the bright and the beautiful—find themselves slipping in international competitions. Despite how hard they work, despite how much they memorize, despite how long they study, despite how much they want to do well.

Maybe what we all need most is time to process what we already know so that we can put it together differently, even more effectively than ever before. Maybe we need to think a bit, out on a porch in a summer breeze, down by the creek when the trout are running, back in the garden when it's time to put the beets and beans in again.

Turn off the television and read a good book. Quit texting and ride your bike. Close the computer and go to a movie. Don't answer any emails. Don't try to "get ahead." Don't take any callbacks. And during the family dinner, turn off the phone. And when the television is on, watch it instead of talking through it. Reclaim your life, your thoughts, your personality, your friends, your family.

No, the world will not end. And no, the rest of the staff will not get ahead of you. They'll be too tired to even think about catching up.

It's time to sleep in like you did in the good old days. Have a late breakfast. Read the newspapers all day long. Call some friends in for a game of pinochle. And then, on Monday, go back to work—having really gotten away from it all—feeling like what you have to do is really worth doing. As Ashleigh Brilliant says, "Sometimes the most urgent and vital thing you can possibly do is take a complete rest."

As the proverb teaches, "A good rest is half the work." At least, that is, if you really want to be productive.

13

THE TEMPTATION OF SINLESSNESS

One of the few things we can be sure to discover as
life goes by is that perfection is perfectly impossible, if for no other reason than that nobody really knows
what that means. What does it mean to be perfectly honest
when we give false hope to a dying mother? What does it
mean to be perfectly obedient when we kill one person to
save another? What does it mean to be perfectly loving and
care more for one child than the rest of them? What does
it mean to wake up in the middle of the night saying to
ourselves, Why do I always do it wrong?

In fact, St. Augustine, the expert on sin, confession
and repentance, says of it: "This is our perfection: to find
out our imperfections." Imperfection we will have always
with us, it seems. And our most important discovery of it
is within ourselves.

But if that is true, what is sinlessness really all about?

We live life coping with the challenge of becoming the best human being we can be. So what are we looking for? What can we possibly hope to attain? And, most of all, how sinful is sinlessness?

The temptation to perfection is a serious one. It gives the impression that such a thing is possible. And that is a dangerous spiritual condition in which to find ourselves. The problem is that perfection may not be able to be achieved but it is both easily faked and easily surrendered. And all in the name of holiness.

It is very easy to be considered perfect. All we need to do is learn to look good in public. Obey. Defer. Follow. Be quiet. It's a child's trick that too easily turns into an adult lifestyle. We do what the world expects us to do and the reward is instant holiness. We keep the rules of the institution. We defer to the opinions of the right people. We follow the crowd. We say nothing when the world is crying for something to be said.

And before you know it, we think we're sinless, too. "You broods of vipers and whited sepulchers," Jesus says to the officials in town who are only collecting the taxes they've been told to collect, who are only teaching what they're supposed to teach—despite the effects of those rules on the hungry and the lepers, the crippled and the women, the foreigners and the poor.

But there is lurking in this kind of sanctity the very deepest pit of arrogance. Before you know it, we have separated ourselves from "those kinds of people." We consider ourselves authorized to pass out large monogrammed A's for the jackets of women who have had abortions, to hound them in public, to cut off their right to insurance, to ignore their needs for day care and health care and full-salaried jobs. And call ourselves holy for doing so.

We set ourselves up as arbiters of the lives of those who go through life grappling with the very idea of God while we settle for law as a substitute for the God we say is Love. We want capital punishment despite the fact that our scriptures—which we read regularly—are clear: "Vengeance is mine, I will repay," says God. And at night, hot with anger at others, we struggle instead to suppress the memory of our own sins not yet painted on a billboard next to the sins of those we condemn. The state of our own personal lives we conceal while we present to the world around us the false smiles and false morality we reserve for those who bear their own confusion and pain for all the world to see.

The judgments we render to the world on others admit nothing about the violence of the condemnations we issue in the name of God. Anger and self-righteousness are the tools of the trade.

And so we concentrate on sin rather than on holiness. We turn God into a tyrant rather than a lover. We lose the very qualities we say we want. We spew acid on the soul of the world and call it perfection.

We batter people with what they are not to do and call it God's word and God's will and completely forget to teach what must be done instead. The Beatitudes—Jesus's sermon about the other side of the Ten Commandments—we forget to teach and hesitate to risk. After all, mercy, meekness, justice, and, most of all, poverty of spirit don't mix well with persecution, anger, condemnation, perfectionism and religious hubris. In the name of conscience, we lose the very foundation of conscience—the awareness of our own struggles, the sense of our own frailty, the pain of our own woundedness and the limits of our own perfection.

With this kind of religion, there is no room for the love of God. The "love that casts out fear" is long gone. We are harsh on others because, in the center of us where the light shines and cannot be hidden, we do not trust the God we say we serve. It is our own sins for which we fear. It is we ourselves whom we doubt can possibly survive in the presence of a just God. Then, knowing how really weak we are, have been, will be again at the very first opportunity, we do our best for the world by condemning all the rest of those who have not condemned us as we deserve.

That is the fear, the pain, the anguish that comes in the dark of the night to torment us. It is that fear of God that drives us to despair. It is the substitution of the God of Wrath for the God of Love in us. It is the punishment we think we deserve and so project onto others. It is one of the greatest burdens of the human soul, this sense of self-loathing.

And it all comes out of succumbing to the sin of perfectionism, the failure to admit that we are not perfect, the norm of the world, the icon of sinlessness. Our only answer is Augustine: "This is our perfection: to find out our imperfections" so that we never need fear our capacity to sin against God by sinning against others.

14

The Struggle Between Guilt and Growth

Everybody is ashamed of something. I remember, at the age of nine, being left alone in the house of a family friend with one direction: "At three o'clock, Joan," they showed me, "turn this knob on the stove straight up so that the black mark is pointing up to the ceiling." Easy, I thought. "Do you promise to remember?" Of course I would.

It was after 5:00 when I remembered. It was about 5:30 when they returned. The roast was shrunken and black and ugly. Still hot, in fact. I swore I'd turned the oven off at 3:00, that I couldn't imagine how it could have gone on again, that the roast looked exactly like that when I turned it off.

It was only a child's fault, of course. But it heralded the impact on me of all the other choice points that would surely follow in life: the promises, the failures, the lies. It has stayed with me all my life: the failure to keep the promise, the lie that followed the failure. It stung with a poisoned stinger that burned on in me long after the roast was forgotten and the disappointment in the eyes of those who had trusted me had faded.

Most of all, I remember the shame. Not only had I failed, I had lied. I was not the person they had all thought I was. I had put a barrier between me and people I loved. The whole scene became a template for the future. And, surprisingly, a good one.

The lifelong question now became what was worse— having to face the long-term sting of shame or bear the short-term pain of truth. And so began my journey from guilt to growth. It became what the church calls, in its explanation of sin as the reason for the coming of Jesus, "the happy fault." The understanding of sin that comes from careless sinning itself, the necessary fault that turns our lives around, that becomes a wisdom to live by.

As I have sat and listened to people over the years, I have become more and more convinced that everyone deals, sometime in life, with a necessary fault. What's more, I am convinced that most people need the Rubicon of the necessary fault. We must consciously begin to choose the kind of person we want to be in life. Without these choices what actually distinguishes character from happenstance in the human soul?

Most of us are not bank robbers because we have never been left alone in the bank with the vault door open. So are we honest or not? Or are we simply deprived of the opportunity to be the least rather than the most of ourselves?

The question is an important one. Do we call prisoners holy because they simply have no chance to rape and plunder, to assault and torture, to change the company books or counterfeit money? Of course not. On the contrary, we know that holiness depends on choices that have been tested by opportunities.

And, if truth were known, this is the very growth that begins in childhood when the feelings of shame emerge to supersede mere theological truisms or notions of responsibility. It is not the shame of which Jung speaks when he calls it "a soul-eating emotion." It is the kind of shame that challenges us to the fullness of ourselves every moment of our lives. As Louis Kronenberger says, "One of the misfortunes of our time is that in getting rid of false shame we have killed off so much real shame as well."

Indeed, it is shame—a living inner shame, the awareness that we have not lived up to our own moral capacity—that challenges us to scale the very heights of human integrity. And it is that which, when honored, grows in us and eventually turns into holiness.

This consciousness of our own moral immaturity, this commitment to free ourselves from particular obsessions with the self, is the ultimate lesson of life. This is the time of the breaking of the chains. It is the moment in which we look into ourselves and concede—to the self—the motives and aspirations and behaviors of which we're really made. Then, purged of the need to pose as some charade of a divinized self, we can finally really begin to grow.

Now, at this acme of self-knowledge, all things are possible and all things are clear. But, however important a time of life it may be, it is not an easy time. There is no soul-suffering more keen than the admission of my humanity to myself: that I am not the perfect parent, that I am not the most responsible employee, that I not the most generous giver, that I am not the most selfless of the group.

And yet, this suffering is not a mortal illness; this suffering of honest self-awareness is an invitation to spiritual rebirth. This is the suffering of which the Sufis speak when they say, "Suffering is a device to turn one's thoughts in the direction of God." Having broken the bonds of delusion, we can at last open the self to the inbreaking of God. And shame, remember, has been the bridge to it.

What's more, once we have faced our inner weaknesses, once we have admitted that what we said we were we have not always been, we come fully alive to ourselves as well as to others. The soul can sing. Now I have begun to grow into the fullness of integrity, into the real richness of the self. Now I am capable of anything because I am no longer a slave to my own delusions. I am free to try and fail, to compete and lose, to know what I can do and surrender what I cannot to those who can. I no longer need to be seen as anything I am not. More than that, I am happy with who I am now ready to become. I do not need to be who I am not. My struggling, honest self is enough for me.

What greater moral stability than that can there possibly be? As George Soros says, "Once we realize that imperfect understanding is the human condition there is no shame in being wrong, only in failing to correct our mistakes." Then there is no such thing as real failure anymore.

15

THE CREATIVITY OF CONFUSION

The story is told that when the home of Pablo Picasso, the great neo-expressionist painter of the twentieth century, was burgled, Picasso told the police that he would paint them a picture of the intruder. "And on the strength of that picture," the French police reported later, "we arrested a mother superior, a government minister, a washing machine, and the Eiffel Tower."

It is possible that never has a clearer word been spoken about the tense and tender relationship between confusion and creativity. Chaos is its own kind of order. Creativity is what a person makes out of the confusion. This emerging new order, forged out of disarray and shaped into vision, defies the future. In the end, creativity develops another glimpse of life previously unknown, perhaps, even to the person who manages to create it.

At the same time, confusion is something our highly technological world wars against. Technology exists to assert the assumption that everything must have a visible function. That the function must be precisely defined. That the precision must be productive. And that the productivity must contribute even more to the order of the world around it. It is an orbit in a circle that maintains a cosmology that can be comprehended—tolerated, in fact— only by the creation of more order.

Except that confusion is part of the process of creation and so cannot, dare not, be lost in some kind of mad service to order. No less a scientist than Albert Einstein himself has confirmed the process: "I used to go away for weeks," he said, "in a state of confusion."

How can what appear to be two completely irreconcilable approaches to life possibly be the answer to each other? Because confusion is a beautiful thing without which no greater beauty can possibly be imagined. Confusion simply upends the expectations that form the steel frames of our lives. "Creativity," Versace says, "comes from a conflict of ideas."

Confusion happens when the frames of our lives, the certainties on which we have come to depend, begin to break down. Nature does not act the way we think it should. What used to be clear to us—the rationales that had kept our lives in place for years—become gray and murky. Worse, our notions about morality, artistic taste, social systems, scientific theories, one or all of the givens in life, lose their previously unchallenged place in our private, internal universe. The ways we have been taught to view the world, to make things happen, to put life together, to accept as the norms of human existence become, for whatever reasons, fallible to the point of mere mist on our old selves. Then, it is necessary to rethink everything. As Erich Fromm says, "Creativity requires the courage to let go of certainties." Then we begin, in confusion, to seek a new order of the heart and the mind and the soul.

Then we are ready to make our small world new again. Purple and yellow are no longer a forbidden color scheme, however out of style it might be right now; interracial marriage is no longer unthinkable; cars with wings are debuted at automobile shows.

Confusion stirs the habitual order of things. It throws the deck of lifestyle cards into the air and puts them back together again. Newly.

The chaos of thought rankles the soul in the middle of the night, forcing us to face the upheaval around us. It forces us finally to ask ourselves, How can we possibly survive this latest assault on the past? with a heart pried open by virtue of the fact, if nothing else, that we can no longer escape it.

When the structures of the past no longer satisfy, no long serve to make life lively, we must now begin to ask new questions and to create new answers to old questions. We have been given cosmic permission to think differently. In fact, we are required to rethink everything once we have begun to rethink anything. It is a no-holds-barred moment in life out of which have come some of the greatest additions to the social order the world had ever imagined: Picasso, for instance; airplanes and floating hotels; heart transplants and women priests; manned air flights to Mars.

Certainty dies in the mist of these new questions. New data, demanded by the new questions, turn the world upside down—like the Kinsey Report, the atomic bomb, feminism, desegregation, transgenderism. And creativity—an attempt to put things back together again but in whole new ways—touches every dimension of the human condition. Art thrives, human relationships change, classism dies, national boundaries begin to seep.

We look at our lives now and as the poet says, "We see it again for the first time."

Confusion becomes the dream state of the awakened mind. The fragments of life, scattered now in broken and bizarre ways, can be restructured in freakish new ways, the results of creativity in every field. Like Picasso's mother superior, government minister, washing machine and Eiffel Tower, the shakeups of our lives settle into a fresh and dynamic way of seeing the world.

So the marriage of confusion and creativity is the beginning of new life. We start now from places we have never been allowed to imagine before and out of them we can imagine new conclusions, as well.

It is the dream state of the soul reaching for new heights, new understanding, new insights into what it might mean to be alive in different and more productive and more provocative ways—which in their turn will also grow old and worn and overdone and so, eventually, prompt their own demise and their own resurgence.

It is the symphony of resurrection played over and over in us, every day of our lives. As Daisaku Ikeda puts it, "You must not for one instant give up the effort to build new lives for yourselves. Creativity means to push open the heavy, groaning doorway to life."

16

THE SANITY OF IRRATIONALITY

All parents drum ideas into their children's heads and all children remember them forever, however hard they tried to ignore them as they heard them. As in, "Too much speed, too little progress" or "Don't eat that, I just bought it!" My own mother's favorite was "Joan, think!" It was a mantra in my house. When I put a blouse on a hanger backward, it was "Joan, think!" If I spelled an "ei" word "ie," it was "Joan, think!" Years later, if I turned north instead of south in the car, it was "Joan, think!" If it was a life question that demanded some kind of wisdom for an answer, it was "Honey, just think a little harder; the answer will come to you."

So pervasive was the idea that thinking was the answer to everything in life that years later, when I was trying to configure a screen saver for my computer, I found myself using three-inch-high letters to inscribe across my desktop, "Joan . . . think!"

The great god of rationality ruled life—in school, at home, in religion, in those terrible word problems in arithmetic, in relationships and certainly in the kind of decision making across the years that would surely change life. Living the right life depended on getting the right answer to everything: where to go, what to do, whom to go through life with, when to make a move, why to bother.

Except that it didn't. All the thinking in the world did not save me from buying the wrong kind of gifts, or going to the party with the wrong people, or accepting the wrong invitation or taking the wrong course or ordering the wrong thing off the menu. Surely there was something else to life besides reason.

I had friends who did all those things and seemed to truly enjoy talking about their mistakes. I watched other people laugh about the bends in the road of life that had led them to one dead end after another. I found out that one bad decision is often more enlightening than what the "right" one would have been. I found out that dating the wrong person does not signal the collapse of a person's social life. Clearly there is something other than rationality that is required if life is ever to have the spice and flavor, the nudge and nonsense that real living brings with it.

The interesting thing is that I found the missing link where I least expected it. One day, out of the blue, I went out and got a bird. I'd owned two large dogs years before, an Irish setter and a golden retriever, both of whom I loved. I'd even had a parakeet and a small conure, one of the smaller species of parrots, for a couple of years. The dogs were amiable, trainable, easily satisfied, submissive.

The little conure was simple, self-absorbed, predictable. The new bird, the caique, which I was sure would be more of the same, suddenly turned my world upside down.

She didn't do rational. She did love. She did play. She did experience. She did energy and curiosity and boundlessness. She did not stay where she was put. She did not eat on Tuesday what she had inhaled on Monday. She could not be bought off. She was a bird with a mission: try everything, go everywhere, seduce everyone. Life to Lady had its own rationality made up of its own crooked lines to whatever it was she wanted. She was impervious to data and dedicated to fun. If she fell off the cage trying to reach for the yogurt dish on the table, she simply got up, fluffed herself off and merrily crawled up someone's pant leg to try again.

I learned from Lady that life was too short to get in a rut. Ruts might be rational but they were highly stultifying, as well. Lady didn't care about right or wrong. She cared about doing. It didn't matter to her if something was on the schedule, carefully thought out, reasonably arrived at. What mattered was doing it and then deciding if it was worth doing again.

She didn't shy away from people to protect herself from life. She went out to life with all the energy she had. Strangers were a challenge, not a threat. There was nothing so important that she wouldn't stop for a cuddle on the way to doing it. There was nothing so necessary that she wouldn't take another road to get to it, just for the sake of trying a new path.

Because of her, I myself began to see life in a very different light. No, pets are not the acme of human life but they do have the capacity to make human life more human. They simply refuse to allow us to see life as solely, only, fundamentally, rational.

Pets teach us to play, to live our own lives more freely. They bring experience where only thought has been. They plague administrators to put their administration down for a little while, to air their souls and learn that things can always be done in more ways than one.

They teach us to love and enjoy things we have never taken the time to see before: A string on a plant leaf becomes a delight, a mirror on a stick becomes a love affair, a toilet paper roll becomes a valuable piece of machinery. Life becomes an adventure rather than a math problem. People become potential friends rather than potential enemies. Every day becomes another possibility to do things differently, do them better, do them often, do them with abandon.

"Until one has loved an animal," Anatole France wrote, "a part of one's soul remains unawakened." It is the awakening of that soul that is really the only really rational thing about being alive.

17

The Loss of the Masculine Emasculates the Feminine

The average advert of the Western world tells the whole story. Women are voluptuous, or weak and curvaceous, or—according to the more pious ones—motherly, nurturing, protective, and self-sacrificing. Always self-sacrificing.

What women face, in the midst of what the human race has long known as a "man's world," is the obligation to propagate, to care for, to sustain the other half of the human race. They are just what it seems a good human being should be. Provided, of course, that they are at all times, and in all situations, quiet about it.

The problem is that for some reason, the formula has never really worked. In every generation women, unlike the template, have emerged full of life and zesty about it, bright and visionary, clear and confident. These women, churchmen, statesmen and insecure men declared, were to be put in their "place." Churchmen theologized female inferiority, philosophers explained female inferiority, and small-souled men of every ilk enforced male domination and took their own superiority for granted, as a result.

The great iconic model, of course, on which they built the notion of female inferiority, irrationality and subservience was Eve, mother of the human race, first woman, spouse of Adam. His nemesis. His failed partner. His weaker side. The one whose "sin" had upended the history of humanity, made it a tale of disgrace and women the very eidolon of distrust. And all of this despite the even greater declaration of the same Hebrew scriptures that both females and males were "made in the image of God."

Public myths, jokes, and wisdom stories have all enshrined the fantasy of female disrepute so that women might never be foolish enough to suspect the slander of it all. "There are three ways to send a message," the old saw taught. "You can telephone, tell a friend or tell a woman." Or advice to men taught that "If a man steals your wife the best revenge is to let him keep her." Or better yet, as F. Scott Fitzgerald writes in *The Great Gatsby,* "I hope she'll be a fool. That's the best thing a girl can be in this world—a beautiful little fool."

Girls got those messages—and denied every one of them.

For centuries, the attempt to define women has been a losing task. Era after era women had to be told again and again what they were supposed to be, what Creation had created them to be, how their position in life was domestic. Female. Secondary. "Helpmates" of men as translators of Genesis in the Hebrew scriptures put it. And that despite the fact that in the over thirty other places the Hebrew phrase *ezer kenegdo* was used in scripture, the words the writers used were always translated "a power equal to" rather than "a helpmate for."*

For centuries, up to our own time, women have been trained to be docile, meek, quiet, and nonthinking bearers of the human race. They were considered the appendages of men who had defined themselves the crown of creation.

But women did not surrender the fullness of their humanity easily, without a struggle.

Women also claimed the active, thinking properties of humanity that men had long claimed as sole owners and called masculinity. Until eventually, everywhere, the denial of the intellectual, spiritual, leadership capacity of womanhood became the chicanery that fooled few any longer. Instead, women emerged over and over again, from one side of the world to the next, as rational, powerful, thoughtful, talented, spiritual, and effective human beings. Just like men.

A list of the "Ten Most Important Women in History" is nothing but a sampling of growing lists of women from every country in the world now being recognized everywhere in the world. All of them unsung for ages but now hailed everywhere, not as the exception to the rule, but the very rule of nature itself.

---

* P. David Freedman, "Woman, a Power Equal to a Man," *Biblical Archeology Review* 9 [1983]: 56–58.

The lists are legendary. James Frater's list of the "Top Ten Greatest Women in History" is only one of many, but it demonstrates the involvement of women in every major human activity throughout time. He cites: #10. Emmeline Pankhurst, 1858; #9. Boudica, 60 CE; #8. Catherine of Siena, 1347; #7. Eva Peron, 1919; #6. Rosa Parks, 1925; #5. Tomyris, c. 6 BCE; #4. Hatshepsut, 1479 BCE; #3. Joan of Arc, 1412; #2. Florence Nightingale, 1820; #1. Catherine the Great II, 1729.

Or more telling yet, of the "Top Ten Most Influential People in History," as defined by the *Historical Atlas of the Mediterranean,* there is only one woman, Olympe de Gouges. But she's on the list because she wrote "The Declaration of the Rights of Women and Female Citizens" in 1791.

The choices may be arguable but the choosing is not.

Scholars now compete to create lists of great women that stretch across every culture on the planet. All of these women were once condemned to the anonymity of history. Now all of them have risen again in our times as signs of the underdeveloped half of the human race whose gifts have, regardless, lived throughout time.

Yet, tragically, still in our own era, women are two-thirds of the hungry of the world. Women remain two-thirds of the illiterate of the world. Women are still the poorest of the poor. On what grounds shall we continue to ignore, suppress, and deny the gifts of women? On what grounds, social, scientific, or theological, shall we seriously argue as long as we do it, that we are fully human, rational, wise and visionary ourselves?

The truth, we know, is that women are not meant to be "female females." They were born to be fully functioning co-creators of the human race, of human civilization, of human equality. Just like their brothers. To deny them the masculine or active side of their humanity is to deny them humanity to the full.

18

The Need for the Feminine in Masculinity

Everyone knew the boy was different, most of all his father. Small for his age, Rob loved the piano and hated football. Fortunately, his father took care of that. He insisted that he play football "no matter how much it hurt." After all, he said, he wanted Rob "to be a man." But Rob who headed his class but was physically too small to ever shine in anyone's sports arena could never hope to meet the standard, either his father's or society's in general. He suffered all his life from the lack of physique, of brawn, of dominance and so, of course, the male swagger that came with them.

The painful awareness of his difference from most of the boys in the neighborhood dashed the father's expectations and deepened the son's dark sorrow.

It is a burden borne silently by more men than most men admit.

The signature behaviors we have been taught to think of as essential to being seen as "manly men" and "feminine females" are, in large part, bogus. What we have been taught as essentially male and female behaviors are learned behaviors, not our innate characteristics.

I saw a picture gallery of men taken the moment they each got a first look at their newborn babies. The tenderness in those eyes, the tears they shed, the awe and awareness of the ecstasy of fatherhood they reported brought the world clock to a stop. This was not male indifference or detachment or distance. And all the while, under it all, the common feeling they reported was, "Now I am a man."

No swagger here, no chest thumping, no affected distance from what is "woman's business." No, human disassociation is not innate to what it means to be masculine. Instead, it's what we each bring to the common project of being full human beings which gives us the gifts that, if allowed to develop, will become the measure of what it really means to be man or woman. To limit either is to damp the full development of both.

The sorry truth is that the world bequeaths standards to us that are ancient and unproven, hostile and exclusive, unfriendly but determinative. What has "always been" takes on the aura of truth and requires us to commit ourselves to maintaining the system that spawned them: the monarchy, for instance; rugged individualism, for instance; social stratification, for instance—like men over women, women over children, and children over small bugs. However useless or illogical those standards may be.

The fact is that everyone is different, all of us someplace along the continuum that runs between totally masculine—whatever that is—and totally feminine. But we're only now, as a people, beginning to accept that fact. We have been told and we have learned the lesson well: It is emotionally, physically, psychologically dangerous not to meet the pattern.

So we go through life dealing with the underlying question that rages on in us: Who am I—really? we wonder. How am I meant to behave?

The movement away from reductionist notions of tribe and clan and nationality to concentration on ideas of what it is to be a person, an individual, unique, rather than one among many, has been a long, hard, slow one in human history. Issues of what it means to have a soul, to accrue human knowledge, or, on the contrary, to be outside the norm of normal human behavior—to be mentally ill or mentally challenged—became subjects of human research, philosophy and concern as long ago as fifteen hundred years before the Common Era. Philosophy and medicine led the pursuit of these questions, but religion and custom, fear of ghosts and hints of a netherworld led to resistance. For centuries, the practices of vivisection, dissection and embalming that offered other ways of bringing physical data to the discussion of what it means to be human were suspect or routinely forbidden in large parts of the Western world.

So, the questions lingered and grew but fear rather than fact ruled the day.

Psychological study of feelings and personality, of human needs and emotions, of the nature of maleness and femaleness, of personhood, of human "normalcy" and fundamental pathologies came late to the party, less than one hundred years ago. Exactly what it is that makes us all the same and yet all different both drives us and escapes us at the same time. And yet, even now, the question of what it means to be an "individual" has yet to be defined definitively.

The question haunts us from dawn to dusk, from night to day. Exactly what is a woman? What is a man? Or better yet, what is a "real woman" and a "real man"? And whatever the answers, how do we show it?

The issues that characterize this problem of identity are more than simple scientific ones. They are socially cataclysmic. Everywhere children learn young that invisible social barriers separate them from the fullness of themselves.

Males—boys, in particular, who do not epitomize definitions of the manly man—who suppresses emotion, exudes physical prowess, and emphasizes sexual conquest—are excluded from contemporary social life for reasons far beyond their control.

They are small boys who play with dolls—and are laughed at for doing it. They are young male teenagers who prefer to learn to knit or dance or sing rather than be athletes and so are hounded to an early grave because of it. They are grown men hiding the truth of their sexual identity from their mothers who want them to get married and produce grandchildren. Or they are young males hiding their softness from fathers who want them to drink hard and kill animals, rather than write poetry or join the local theater group. They are men who learn to feel diminished by doing "women's work" like babysitting or child care. They are grown men who grow up full of self-hatred for not being muscle-bound and autocratic, loud and overpowering of others, sure of themselves, demeaning of others, rough and tough and controlling.

They are men with sensitive hearts who love to hold their children, who kiss their sons and teach them to cook, who encourage their daughters to greatness, who have no expectations of being waited upon by women who have full lives of their own to live.

And yet they spend their lives questioning their identity to the point that the questions themselves are madness-making. Only when we all come to the point where "masculinity" can claim for itself the kind of feminine freedoms to love and cry and care which the psychologist Carl Jung speaks about can men become the fullness of the real man they are meant to be. It can only happen when the rest of us begin to realize that the questions we've been asking about what it means to be a fully developed person are themselves wrong.

The great question of life is not so much, What is it to be masculine or what is it to be feminine? The great question of life is, What is it to be human? Then, the humanity of all of us will be safe. Then the humanization of the human race will really be possible.

19

The Liberation in Loss

Loss is part of life. It's just difficult to know when loss is really loss or gain come from another direction. The examples are legion.

"Every night," the woman told me, "I wondered if tomorrow would be the last day." Her young middle-aged husband had suffered for years with myocardiopathy; at this point he was bedridden twenty-four hours a day with no heart transplant in sight. She had raised the kids, held down the job, nursed him through it all. The very thought of losing him was more than she could bear.

Carl saw it happen to other people but he never thought it could possibly happen to him. Wall Street CEOs of much bigger companies than his had already been removed, yes, but they were the culprits, not he. "I didn't leave the company," he said later. "The company left me." He was devastated by it. He got other job offers, of course, but refused them all. The very thought of going through it all again somewhere else was simply too much for him to risk.

After years in the ministry, after years of struggle, Val left it, sure of only one thing: However foolish it may be to leave it with nothing to go to, it was even more foolish for people to stay where they knew they did not belong. The spiritual dimensions of life had grown ever stronger over the years but the struggle to manage the poles of the institution had simply become too complex to think of spending a lifetime doing it.

In all three cases, and in hundreds—thousands—of variations of them, the loss was major. It was also unavoidable and permanent. For none of them was it easy to lose what they thought they would never lose. Nor was it something that any of them had at all foreseen.

It was simply that other piece of life, the unknown part, the one unplanned and unwanted that had intruded on their perfect worlds to require a new decision from each of them. Marriage was forever, she was sure. The company was sound, he was sure. The ordination was of God's design; surely God would sustain it. And yet all of them knew, those days, those fidelities were over now.

But all of them had been mistaken. And all of them went through what were, for them at least, cataclysmic losses.

Whatever the nature of the loss—death, status, circumstances—the pain of it feels almost surgical. Sometimes we lose things we had. Sometimes we lose what we wanted but could not have, like a child or a place in the system we value so much. Sometimes we mourn what we never had and go to cement simply waiting for what will never come. Whatever the nature of the loss, it leaves a vacuum in the heart. Despite the fact that she had taken care of her invalid husband for years, the widow felt abandoned. Carl felt betrayed and angry for having trusted the company with his life. Val felt bereft, misunderstood, cut off from a spiritual bloodline.

The fact is that when we lose a piece of ourselves—a marriage, a family, a defining institution, the kind of status or stability we have depended on this person, this place to give us—we lose a much larger part of our identity than we ever realized was possible. Not to be Mrs., not to be Sir, not to be Reverend—not to be the person on the block everyone knows, the tenant in the building who has the best job, the one in the office who does all the computer work, the one in the parish everyone depends on to chair the festival, not to be the "One who" is important to everyone around them anywhere they are is a mighty loss. Then the question screams into the night: Who am I now? Is this all there is?

The very thought of losing those things is enough to wake a person up in a cold sweat in the middle of the night.

And yet, there is a resurrection that comes with loss. People can no longer see in us the person they saw before, true. But that is one of the gifts of loss. Loss frees us to begin again, to be seen differently, to tap into something inside of ourselves that even we were never really sure was there. But, whether we knew it or not, did badly want.

We can now—perhaps must now—be ourselves but in some very different ways. We don't have to go on making a success of the family business. Or even being Mrs. Anybody. Or being called upon so often for the same things in life that we never get to show the world that we can do other things, as well. No doubt about it: Loss is liberation time.

Then we must begin even to know ourselves differently—as more than the mother or the son, the doorman or the doctor or the groundskeeper or the mail carrier. Now we have to dig deep inside us to find out what other parts of ourselves are waiting to be discovered.

It's when we hunker down inside ourselves at a time of great loss—withdrawing from the world, refusing to bloom again some other place—that the loss stands to destroy us. When we walk through the door of loss we find it always open. The only problem lies in whether or not we take that first step over the doorsill.

It is, of course, possible to freeze in place. We can simply sit our lives away waiting for someone to discover what we were and want us to be it again. The problem is that, unknown even to ourselves, perhaps, it wouldn't be possible even if we tried. We can't simply go back to being what we were before. Everything has changed. The situation is new. The life demands are new. And we are new now, too. We know what it is to be wrenched out of the only self we have ever really known, the one we thought we would be forever. Most of all, we know more about life and more about ourselves now. We are meant to go on, yes—in fact, we have no choice—but we are meant to go on differently. As Heraclitus of Ephesus said, "No one ever steps in the same river twice." Life moves inexorably on.

At the end of the day, though, one thing has become painfully, positively clear: Loss is not loss. It is simply the invitation to find the more of ourselves that is waiting to become the rest of ourselves.

"Success," Winston Churchill said, "is bounding from failure to failure with no loss of enthusiasm." And Churchill should know. He began government service in England as lord of the admiralty, lost that post, regained it, became prime minister, lost that post, regained it, and lost it again. Losing is clearly part of life. Sometimes its most arduous part, but never its most destructive part.

If anything, loss is not meant to ruin us or our sleep for the rest of our lives. It simply prepares us to lose better the next time, to go into life over and over again, knowing full well that this phase, too, will end so that we can take our own unbounded enthusiasm into the next part of coming to wholeness. Whatever that may be.

20

LONELINESS: AN INVITATION TO DISCOVER NEW RESOURCES

It happened long years ago but in lonely times even now I still cling to it as the icon of possibility, a real lifeline through loneliness both then and now. I was a very young nun then, in my first teaching situation—a rural one—and living with sisters who had been in the community for years, many of them in their sixties. Unlike me at the age of nineteen, they were all professed nuns. I was a scholastic, a student nun. I didn't know any of them personally, we had nothing in common, and community customs simply did not provide for any way to make personal connections. In fact the rules said that professed sisters were not permitted to speak to the nonprofessed except professionally. It was a very lonely, very desperate kind of time. At that age, at a new point in life, I needed more personal contact than that. I began to wonder if I would really be able to get through it.

I couldn't leave the place. I couldn't change the place. I could only get more and more dour by the day. The question plagued me: I was surely not the first person who had ever been in a situation like this, so was I suffering from loneliness or self-pity?

Clearly, getting through this was up to me.

I knew that I had to have a plan. So, I made a list of things I had wanted to do for years but was never in the right situation to try. In any other circumstances, I would never even have had the time to pursue them: study all of Shakespeare's plays, for instance, read all the American musicals, learn to carve leather. But here and now, once my lessons were prepared, I could suddenly be totally immersed in a life that was educational, artistic, even relaxing. It became a time of my life that I have always looked back on with real satisfaction and even a bit of nostalgia.

As a result of that situation, however, I discovered something that has proven invaluable over the years. In order for loneliness—as real as it is—to deplete us, we must feed it.

Loneliness is the perfect setup for self-pity. No one comes to see me; pity me. No one asks how I'm doing; pity me. No one invites me out; pity me. But that's only the beginning of the problem. Not only do others not see the problem or do anything to address it, but I don't do anything for me either.

We simply withdraw within ourselves to confirm our misery. Withdrawal itself becomes our only response to an already barren environment. Now there is nothing but emptiness outside and emptiness of our own making inside, as well. There is nowhere to go but further down, both psychologically and spiritually.

But loneliness is another kind of call to go on growing in ways that take us beyond dependency on others to the creation of life's most important resources within ourselves.

Loneliness is a sign that there are whole parts of us that cry out for development. After all, we are meant to be more than our social lives. We are meant to have inner lives that are themselves rich and satisfying. It is a matter of learning how to become good company for ourselves. We are not meant to lie awake at night wondering if someone, anyone, will come to our rescue. We are meant to be our own best friends.

And at that point, I am the only one who can rescue me. The others can accompany me. They can look out for me. They can offer me their support and understanding and care. But if there is something missing in my life, I'm the only one who really knows what it is. I am the only one who can put it there.

Every life deals with loneliness at some point or other: Our partner dies; sickness sets in that makes the old social calendar impossible; we find ourselves in a new job, a new town, a new country, a new world. More than one person who was once naturally outgoing and apparently self-confident has succumbed to all of those things. The problem is that the more we withdraw, the more withdrawn we become. People stop calling. No one stops by. I never meet anyone new. I never do meaningful new things. But then is not the time to hide from the world; then is the time to strike out in totally new ways to find the rest of the self in the rest of the world.

It is the opportunity we do not seek, to do things we

never thought of doing, and in the end it is an invitation to become new again.

This is the moment the old frame cracks, the old certainties fail, the old patterns and habits and social clubs disappear. The tried-and-true are not only useless now, they are simply gone. The only possibility for emotional survival lies at a time like this in going out into a totally strange place, trusting ourself to new people. Not to burden them but to learn from them. It means that we must do something we have never done before—join a book club or a quilting group or deliver trays for Meals on Wheels— anything that provides structure and regularity until, suddenly, we have a new circle of friends to help us plan our own time differently.

But loneliness is about more than simply figuring out how to use time while we try to forget the pain that comes when we're at loose ends. It is also a call to make other people's needs our own. What we learn in loneliness is that everybody needs someone. The question at a time like this, then, is, Who needs something I can do for them? It's time to get involved with someone else's emotional support in addition to my own. Which is why, perhaps, so many people who lose a loved one begin groups to support people in similar situations.

Loneliness is not the end of anything. It is the starting point at which we are able, this time, to choose fresh ways of being alive. It's like being dropped down on the Planet Nowhere and told that you can do anything you'd like to do. And for the first time in your life, you must and you do.

Most of all, loneliness is not a call for other people to

take care of us. Loneliness is the call to ourselves, now that we have acquired a better understanding of it so well, to do something to alleviate the loneliness and needs of others. Dag Hammarskjöld had a keen understanding of an affliction of the soul that easily keeps us awake at night and feeling hollow during the day. "Pray that your loneliness," he said, "may spur you into finding something to live for, great enough to die for."

21

THE SEEDS OF LOVE IN FRIENDLESSNESS

Love is good for greeting card companies. People everywhere—even people in other parts of the world now—send cards. The cards say: "Miss you," "Wanting you," "Grateful for you," and, of course, "Love you"— especially on Valentine's Day. The question worth thinking about, of course, is, Who sends them, who gets them, what do they mean by them—and, perhaps even more important, who doesn't get them or send them and what does that mean, too?

There is, after all, a kind of cachet about being above it all, about not bothering about such things. About not being entangled. Then, it would seem, you can go to bed at night emotionally independent. Free. Unaccountable to anyone else's agenda. Unaccountable to anyone else's needs. Carefree and careless. "I'm my own person," they put it, as if that were some kind of personal achievement, one of the great triumphs of existence, to have no sense of accountability or responsibility or enduring affection for anyone but the self.

The irritating question, the question that rankles the soul, however, the question that can really make a person uneasy in the still of a friendless night, is the obvious one: Now that you are free, what has your freedom gotten you?

In the answer to that question lies a wisdom that little else in life can garner. It takes a long look into a mirror to even approach the depths of it.

On the surface, loners are a rare breed. Almost everyone looks as if they are attached to someone somehow. As best friend or confidant. As lover, partner, or spouse. But as Eric Hoffer puts it, "We lie loudest when we lie to ourselves." These so-called connections are often only a superficial patina on the social dimensions of life. They mask as the real thing. But real relationships require commitment and concern, affection and truth, independence as well as support. Loners are the friends who come to all the parties but who are never around when they're needed.

To be a loner with a mask is a precarious situation. There are learnings to be had here, all of them the hard way.

Loners soon discover, when they find themselves confronted with the big things of life—debilitating sickness, great loss, death, a plundered heart, a deep disappointment—how much there is that cannot be done alone in life. There are some things only friends can do for us: understand our grief, sustain our despair, pick up our load, be a light in our darkness. Without that kind of intimacy and confidentiality, we are left alone to smolder in the pain of it all. We become more prone to try to anesthetize what we cannot resolve. In that event, we are left with two problems where only one had been before.

The illusion of self-sufficiency is a very serious emotional barrier to being able to negotiate the real tasks of life. It denies us the gift of criticism: There is no one to tell us what we need to know, and no one we are willing to listen to. We isolate ourselves from the very things we need to plot the success we seek.

All the intellect, all the skill in the world, cannot substitute for the fine art of human relationships which, in the end, are what we need most to steer us through life, steady our steps, and carry us over the boulders that block it. Self-love is a sterile relationship at best. How do we learn to love others without the model of those who love us? Where do we turn to understand life when we have exhausted our own resources, but have failed to attach ourselves to the resources of others to complement our own? To make ourselves our own god is to worship a puny god indeed.

From those seeds—a growing awareness of personal incompleteness, insufficiency of soul, the limitations of self-love and the deficiency of our own personal resources—evolve the ability to love beyond narcissism. It leaves us standing stripped of our pretenses and vulnerable to the rest of the world. Love stretches us beyond ourselves and stretches the soul toward inclusiveness. It makes us equal parts of the human race with all the strength and all the weakness, all the good and all the frailty that brings.

We gain the insight to see ourselves through the friendships we make. They mirror us to ourselves. In them we see clearly what we do not have as well as what the world cannot do without. They do not judge us or condemn us or reject us. They hold us up while we grow, laughing and playing as we go. They bring us to the best of ourselves. "One's friends," George Santayana wrote, "are that part of the human race with which one can be human."

Friends enable us to know and to accept our own deep needs and so understand and support the needs of others. They bring us home to ourselves and to the rest of the world at the same time. To be in relationship with someone is to open ourselves to becoming more than we can possibly be alone. Then, when that happens, the long nights of wondering, as one more night slips by, what it is that can possibly be missing in life while we touch the empty spot in the heart are over now.

Then when the birthdays come and the anniversaries pile up and Valentine's Day comes again, we not only send cards, we will also get them.

22

THE LONELINESS OF LOVE

The ads are everywhere. The Internet pours them out in multiple millions: fifteen ways to get him to date you, twelve ways to tell if she is the one for you, ten ways to get your love to marry you, eight ways to get your partner's attention. There's no end to the lists or the numbers. The only thing wrong with any of them is that they are all selling a bogus product. There are no ways at all to make anyone notice you, love you, choose you, understand you or stay with you, short of physical captivity, of course—and that's illegal.

The truth is that love is a very individual thing, a very personal reaction, a very unique relationship. All the tricks in the social repertoire without the chemistry that makes the relationship unique will not work. And that's not foolproof either. Natural attraction brings people together, yes, but it does not promise to keep people together.

Even when people stay together forever, there is little proof that they completely understand each other or can really hear the other person's pain, or want the same things or perceive the world in the same way and from the same perspective.

Nor can love ever assure two people that they are totally in sync. On the contrary: If anything is difficult, it seems, it is couples' communication of any kind—in professional comradeships, in long-standing friendships, in married couples. Psychologists and counselor types devote entire workshops to it. They develop therapy sessions to guide couples through it, or at least cure them of their false hopes. They fix what the ads imply should really be natural to us all.

But, if forming couples is natural, if coming to love another person is important, staying in love—in communion, in community—is hard work. No one is an island, the poet John Donne told us. And that's true. But no one is a copy of anybody else either.

The ads that promise eternal bliss, perfect coupledom and a sense of total communion with another human being—with any other human being—have a truth-in-advertising problem. Not only are such relationships rare, they are for the large part impossible. And that's good. Otherwise we wouldn't have couples at all. We would just have bad copies of the one who is the real person, the dominant person, in this relationship. Then, one person's tastes, goals, agendas take precedence, eclipse often, the plans, hopes and likes of the other. The "couple" becomes one person in charge and the other in a supporting role.

But love is not like that.

Real love is a very lonely venture. We always want more from the other person than we can ever hope to get. And we always give less than is needed or expected, even when we think we're giving everything we have.

Love is not simply coming to be attracted to another human being. In the great eternal cosmology of life, love functions to take us more deeply into ourselves than it can possibly take us into the unknown Other. Love teaches us how really needy we are. Or perhaps, even more impacting, how actually uninterested we are in anyone besides ourselves.

We come to experience the long hard journey from the self to the other. If we're lucky, we come to realize that the purpose of love is to take us out of our own cravings for attention to attend to someone else. And there's the rub. Love is always a matter of getting beyond our perpetual self-talk long enough to read the signs of someone else's need for approval, for care, for attention, for development. It is the measure of our own unselfishness, not simply an assessment of the selflessness of the other.

Loneliness, therefore, is built right into the love relationship. It begins in the loneliness that motivated the search in us for someone to match our lives, in the first place. Then, it comes out of a need to find the one other person in the world who would care enough about the things we care about to accompany us through them.

Love functions in the loneliness that comes from expecting what no one other person can possibly give us—total satisfaction, total presence, total joy and total understanding. The more love we find then, the more loneliness that comes with it. Wanting total absorption of another person defeats the very gifts that real love alone can give—independence, confidence and the courage to be ourselves.

And if it has been love at all, it will leave us alone and lost in the world once again when death closes over the relationship, still searching, still disappointed.

At most, there are two ways that can launch us into an experience of real love.

The first is a journey that takes ruthless self-criticism as its base. It means that, however long this relationship lasts, I must regularly ask myself whether or not I am really attending to the other. Do I hear the other and, most of all, do I respond? Have I tried to determine what it is that the other needs from me right now and then, if necessary, negotiate the giving of it? Am I really trying to come out of myself for the sake of the other?

The second consciousness of love is that the world is not a world of one—me. Love makes space for the insights of others, for the opinions of others, for the very separate goals and hopes of others who are also struggling both to be themselves and to enable the one they love to do the same.

As Anna Strong writes, "To fall in love is easy, even to remain in it is not difficult; our human loneliness is cause enough. But it is a hard quest worth making to find a comrade through whose steady presence one becomes steadily the person one desires to be."

Love is not a mold that makes two people the same person. Love is the dream that enables both of us to be our own best person—together. Love knows that no one can fill up in us what we lack in ourselves. But coming to live what we know about love for the sake of the other, as well as for ourself, is the one thing that can possibly stop the restless sleep that comes with loneliness.

23

THE FULLNESS OF SEPARATENESS

I am writing this in a tiny stone house at the top of a mountain. The line of sight to the bay below is unmarked by anything of human origin. There are a few sheep curling in and out of the harsh gray boulders that run down to the sea. Nothing else. It is a rare place.

We live in a very full world now and so, reflexively perhaps, cultivate a great, silent fear of the kind of separation a mountain and boulders can bring. We live in a society where houses stand cheek by jowl with other houses and, in apartment buildings, owners are separated from strangers only by one small, dull, gray door. We can drive from one small town to another for miles throughout the country and down the coasts and never know when one ends and the other begins. The major cities of the world and their greater metro areas hold two-thirds of the world's population. They overflow with people. Tokyo, 37 million;

Delhi, 22 million; Mexico City, 20 million; New York, 20 million; Los Angeles, 14 million; Philadelphia and Houston, 5 million; Taipei, 2 million.

Silence is passé in this world. Isolation is impossible. Even to be on the streets in cities like these is a claustrophobic experience. I was caught in a slowly moving whirlpool of people in a blocks-long market in Taiwan one night. I was jostled along in the flow of the crowd, out of touch with the group with whom I'd come, and a bit panicked by the fact that there was apparently no way out of the moving mass. There were no exits, no crossroads, no boulevards, no lanes of traffic. Nothing but a swirl of anonymous humanity and I was being crushed in it.

No doubt about it. Separation—openness—a sense of physical distance between us, is a foreign phenomenon in this world. In this great mass of humanity in which we all now live like robots in motion, like giant power points tethered to an electronic world, we have learned to fear the thought of isolation. It is the abhorrence of being out of touch, alone, in such a world as this that haunts us. And yet, it may be a sense of void we need most if we ourselves are ever really to be full and fresh of soul again.

Trepidation of the hollow places of life underlies almost all of the agonies of soul with which we struggle. The separations that death brings; the separation that moving from one house, one city, one job brings; the separation from family that leaves us with a sense of total unconnectedness, even in the midst of the mass of stifling humanity. It's then, when the world is still, that darkness brings a veritable experience of disconnection to haunt us with the question of whether or not our private little worlds will survive the night. Will life as I know it with all its supports and guides be there for me tomorrow or not?

So full are we of the fullness around us that we miss the fullness of emptiness itself.

So accustomed have we become to the false fullness that comes with noise and the pressure of strange masses of people, the loss of physical space and the mental chaos that comes with unending technological availability, that we have lost our awareness of the gift of disjunction—of a sense of pure selfness—and the genuine fullness of soul it brings.

Separateness, the willingness to live inside ourselves rather than to live off the thoughts and words and chaos and clamor around us, heightens our very awareness of being alive. It brings our senses to the point of dry heat and laser acuity. For the first time, we are free to really see the world in which we live. We can suddenly hear what we have not been able to hear for years—our own thoughts, our personal concerns, our own ideas.

Once we eliminate distractions—idle and empty distractions—we have the opportunity to discover ourselves and all our lacks and limitations, all our strengths and certainties. Now nothing can edit them, nothing can damp them down but ourselves. There's no one else to either edit them or repress them. There is no one whispering in our ear, tugging at our sleeve, insisting that we edit what we think. There is no one else now but ourselves to warn us against the demonic ideas within us.

Out here alone, we can decide to say aloud what, like

sandpaper, scratches at our souls. Or, we can simply exorcise them all ourselves. Out here in the spiritual-psychological desert alone, no one can deny us the right to determine exactly what they are, these words of mine, that may well shake the neighbors, the system, the family. That may well either cost me or cure me of my rejection of the self for the sake of the approval of others. In the emptiness there is only ourselves and the soft, quiet call of the Godness within us to depend on. It is the moment of maturation.

Separation removes us from the turmoil that blocks out both the unfinished business of the past and our own quiet but undeveloped hopes for the future. It is life in the present, whole and entirely our own. It enables us, finally, to ask and receive an answer to the question we fear more than any other: Who would I be if I ever became myself?

We're concentrated now and free of spirit. We can finally be whoever we know to really be ourselves—whoever that is and whatever that means. With our souls focused on our own capacity for life and our senses detoxified of the extraneous, there is space now for newness, for I-ness, for the experience of being totally in charge of my own soul. I can attend it and shape it and claim it as my own.

Otherwise, what is there to depend on in the dark of the night when the questions are clearest and the doubts are close by? "Once conform," Virginia Woolf wrote, "once do what other people do because they do it, and a lethargy steals over all the finer nerves and faculties of the soul. [It] becomes all outer show and inward emptiness; dull, callous, and indifferent."

Dulled by the weight of bearing the ideas of others

rather than creating our own, callous to the meaning of them since we have not thought them through, indifferent to the effects of them since we take no personal responsibility for them, we become a mere shadow of a person, a cardboard cutout of the self. And without the experience of our own emptiness, we do not even know that we have allowed ourselves to become a nonperson. Then, at some crucial moment in our own development we are shocked to realize that we have not taken the time to examine the difference between what we say and what we think. Nor do we pursue the question of why we think what we think let alone of why there is a difference between what we think and what we say.

Unfortunately, when the questions come, in the middle of the night, they come to us. There is no one else there to answer them for us. Then we most need the fullness of the self.

"The best things and best people," the poet Robert Frost wrote, "rise out of their separateness. I'm against an homogenized society because I want the cream to rise."

To think for ourselves, to separate ourselves from the ready-made thoughts around us—at least once a day—is to allow the cream to rise in us.

24

The Call to Solitude in Crowds

The first real jolt of it came on the lake. It was a mild evening, the water was still and shimmering. Every once in a while a fish jumped leaving ripple upon ripple for the world to see. Out near the trench where commercial boats trolled for the next day's catch, I could see a field of small boats settled in to wait with them for the night feeding hours.

Our own boat barely moved in the quiet water. We each sat there in the silence of our selves, comfortable in our own small worlds, staring across the horizon into the declining sun. Every once in a while I heard a single call echo across the lake: "Anything hitting out here?" one voice called. "Yep, the perch," someone called back. Not another word. Not another sound. The perfect night.

And then suddenly someone shattered the sundown like a world full of glass falling down a mountainside. A larger boat came thundering down the lake, its outboard motors roaring. But it wasn't the boat or its wake or the whirr of the motors that broke the night. Up on the bow, three boys sat carrying boom boxes on their shoulders, each of them playing a different piece of hard rock, loud, louder, as loud as it could possibly play. It was the blaring of land-side noise that blasphemed the night. It was the intrusion of one world on another that demonstrated the difference between them.

All that night I heard the sound of the rock beat in my head. All that night I contemplated the place of silence in a world filled with crushing sound.

The world is sopping with sound now. No place is safe from it anymore. It spills out of doorways and down halls and over streets until life itself becomes a cacophony of unrelated sounds. Music plays in doctors' offices. Televisions and computers vie for attention in the same room. Talk shows invade every office waiting room, every taxicab ride, every airport boarding area, every mall and every restaurant. There is simply no place where a person can go and simply enjoy the silence.

And why should we? What good is the vacuum of solitude and silence?

There is a pathology of noise that drips into the soul in contemporary society until the soul simply disappears under the weight of it. Then there is only the shadow of a person left looking for itself. Sound drowns out thought until all we find within ourselves are questions where the cuttings of answers ought to have begun taking root.

The serenity that comes from solitude, in the silent

companionship of the self, fritters away. I have no memory of it. I only know what it means now to race from one group to another, leaving my unfinished self behind or always, always losing another bit of myself to the volume of undigested ideas around me.

The question that rankles the soul is a threatening one: Yes, yes, the soul says, but, in the end, what do I myself think? In fact, do I still think at all?

At night I search the darkness of my soul for other ways to be alive, for other ways to go through time, for other ways to claim my right to discover myself before I allow myself to be bought and sold again to the loudest groups around. In the dark, I wonder what positions to take, what way to go on an issue. And then I realize that I can't make any real choices at all on anything until I have the quiet to consider for myself what I would really think about a thing—if I ever did.

It's in solitude that I decide whether I really like myself or not. It's easy to practice the fine art of fitting in, of course. What is difficult is to learn how to withhold myself from the dictates of the crowd enough before, unconsciously, I become them instead of me. And without even realizing it.

Solitude acquaints us with ourselves, with what we really think and deeply feel. Or, perhaps, do not feel at all. Then, it gives us the time to ask ourselves whether or not we should feel or think anything about this at all.

There are those, of course, who fear the silence of solitude. They find solitude depressing because they have learned to need noise to save them from themselves. For them, solitude has become a great empty space that is full of nothing and gives nothing and promises nothing. But for those who practice the leisure that comes with solitude, solitude is a resting place for the soul. It brings respite, repose, quiescence. It allows the quiet that thinking demands.

Solitude enables us to bask in a world without clamor. It renders us capable of hearing the songs within us, of singing the songs within us, of writing the songs within us that wait to be discovered. It welcomes us to the world of contemplation.

"Language," Paul Tillich wrote, "has created the word loneliness to express the pain of being alone. And it has created the word solitude to express the glory of being alone." That is the kind of glory crowds cannot give us but whose clamor does, indeed, in its own way demand the solitude it takes to be heard.

25

THE EMPTINESS OF CROWDS

I t's easy to talk about "my life." But actually that is only half the truth of what it means to be human. My life is actually lived on a teeter-totter poised somewhere between me and them. And therein lies the tension that so commonly troubles us in the deepest darkness of the night. Too often balancing the two—me and them—is an elusive art.

We love to be told that we are social beings, yes, but we also know deep in the core of us that we are not frantically social beings. Not only do we not need to be around people all the time, but we actually like to be alone much of the time. In fact, we often find life most difficult precisely when we are caught in crowds we cannot escape. The average human being—you and I, perhaps—is, in other words, also very private beings, not reclusively withdrawn but genuinely reserved, reflexively reticent, commonly restrained.

To be lost in a crowd of more comrades than confidants,

where conversation is more small talk than honest discourse, can tire us to the center of our souls. It is time lost in trivia, time taken away from thought. It is time without return of the energy we need to deal with the rest of life thoughtfully, seriously. It barters the serious levels of life for the superficiality of the herd. It forfeits community for the sake of the crowd and crowds bring clutter, bring clamor, bring distraction.

In many ways, crowds do more to take us away from ourselves than they do to nourish us. They survive on the periphery of life and bring little in the way of personal support as communities do. Instead, inchoate crowds bring, at best, the sheer comfort of knowing that I am not standing on the promontory of the world alone.

Crowds swirl us through life, run us from one event to another, looking for faces in the assemblage more familiar than the masses on the street but hardly soul mates. We get caught up in the excitement of a crowd and make the excitement our own. We go with the crowd and come away knowing what the world around us is feeling whether we really feel it or not.

But none of that is enough.

Crowds come in two flavors. One type of crowd, unrelated as it may seem, is driven by a cause, a purpose, a movement that taps into the very depths of our own souls. These crowds magnify our own hopes and goals and concerns in life. All strangers, perhaps, they nevertheless already share some great human hope.

The other type of crowd organizes around nothing for no particular change in the human condition. They share no common reason for being together. They are the gathering at the street dance, the participants in the discussion, the people at the neighborhood barbecue, the onlookers at the rally. They are all there together and we are in the midst of them and we share a common event or conversation. But they are no vehicle for serious thought or significant actions.

Great unrelated groups of people do not tend our pain. They do not heal our souls. They do not bring us to new insights or enable us to understand much more about what is driving the latest social trend than we did before we got there.

Rather, crowds tell us what the undercurrents of life are but they do not tell us where this present controlling undercurrent came from or why it happened or where, if it continues, it will end up. Crowds are amorphous gatherings of strangers in a person's life, not family, not friends. And therein lies the danger. There are no personal ties here that can attest to their integrity, let alone lay claim to their real care for anyone who joins them.

A crowd is simply either the whirlwind or the interest of the moment, not organized movements. They arise out of singular personal interests and disappear when those particular interests disappear. They are at most a gathering of like-minded people connected only by the moment or the character of the event. They are a formless, shapeless population of some aspect of society—the office staff, the fans, the alumni, the neighbors.

The fellow travelers in a crowd do not claim to have a common heart; they simply set out to express a common interest, more or less important, more or less immediate. More important, they can, if allowed—completely unnoted and unnoticed—suck the air out of an individual and turn the average enthusiast into a cipher rather than a person.

Crowds do not give voice to the individual. Instead they suppress it. They demand subservience to the interests of the crowd rather than to the welfare of the individual. They are noisy creatures who for all their show of comity render the individual silent. Most of all, they do not answer the questions that torment us in the middle of the night about what we ourselves really think when we are alone.

But a person cannot be a person unless and until they are free to act beyond, outside and even against the crowd.

Crowds are important in life but they do not constitute the real essence of what it means to be a human being. There are persons, of course, who sublimate themselves to the crowd in order to feel part of something bigger than themselves, to take on an identity that they themselves have not formed yet, to acquire an aura of the power or status of the crowd itself. Those people will never really become persons.

We can take all of our social cues from a passing crowd—like schoolchildren jockeying for social approval. We can learn what clothes to wear there, what people to associate with, what thoughts to think—but we cannot learn to be ourselves or to make any particularly distinct contribution to the rest of the world.

We may find companionship in a crowd. We can look to the crowd for recreation. We can want the fellowship and security of the crowd but we cannot mistake that kind of ephemeral social contact for genuine human love and care, for tested constancy or disinterested concern. We cannot look here for the definition of what we most want to be as a human being and become as a person. Those things we must find for ourselves.

The Greek philosopher Epicurus clearly noted the tension between being a self-defined individual and being lost in the identity of the crowd. His advice to the centuries after him is a somber one. He wrote, "I have never wished to cater to the crowd; for what I know they do not approve, and what they approve I do not know." We can roll and toss over that kind of insight for years but in the end the wisdom of it leaves little room for compromise. What we want to become we must become alone. Only then may we safely give ourselves over to the crowd.

26

THE NOISE WITHIN THE SILENT SELF

"Remember, Joan, you can't ever really run away from anything," my mother taught me. "In the end, you only take yourself with you." At that age, I thought the words were simply a trick of language. Maybe an outworn kind of witticism. It took years before I realized what she had not said, what she had failed to tell me, had instead allowed me to find out for myself. By that time I didn't need to have someone else explain it to me.

I know now that whatever it is that is troubling us is not outside of us. It is inside of us. Rattling around. Muttering. Waking a person up in the dregs of the night. Filling our dreams with specters and sweat. Echoing loudly in the emptiness within us. One great cacophony of internal noise that goes with us wherever we are. Always.

It is that very noise that emerges in babble and prate when we're alone. When it's night. When there is no other noise to drown it out. It is the noise of the agitated soul. It is confusion. Or fear. Or pressure. Or the recurring guilt or aimless pain we do not say to anyone but which weighs us down and fills us up to overflowing.

It is the call to our souls of the unfinished business of our lives, of the tensions we never lifted, the relationships we never resolved, the promises we never kept, the dreams we never achieved, the things we never became, the enmities we never accepted. It is the question of how to live with all those things now that nothing can be done about any of them at all.

Everything else in life is sound. What rises from the inside of us, unbidden and unwelcome, is noise. It curdles our life. And at night it demands our personal attention when we can do nothing about it but cower, knowing all the while that clearing the static of it must be accomplished alone. It's what we don't say in the daytime about what we don't like. It's what wouldn't look good to others if we ever did say it. It's what we don't like about ourselves and do not want other people to sense about the small parts of us.

And yet, this noise in me is the voice of the Spirit calling me to attend to what I have long ignored or denied or forgotten. It is the challenge to face up to the unfinished business of my life. To resolve what I regret. To confront whatever it is that is blocking my ability to live a life free of consternation, alive with joy. Indeed, we can't ever really run away from anything. We can only settle it or be harassed by it all the nights of our life. It is a choice we make that will affect the entire rest of our lives. It is the martial art of the soul.

Silence is the gift that throws us back on ourselves. Which is exactly why there are so many who cannot bear the thought of it. Without external distractions, we are left vulnerable to the voices within that demand that we come to grips with all the pieces of the self we have so carefully concealed. Beneath the smiles and the frowns we use to protect ourselves from anyone who might get too close to the turmoil within us lies the noise of the soul that will not cease until we finally agree to hear it. It is the silent self that calls us to damp the noise that hounds us in the night, that calls us to responsibility for the authenticity of the self.

Internal noise is the eruption of the psyche within, which demands our attention to the submerged parts of ourselves that haunt us yet. Our secret pettiness, perhaps. The new fires of anger or the old fires of depression that rage beneath the patina of patience. The smile that is not real.

The truth is that internal noise is not meant to burden us. It's meant to enable us to go on with new energy, new honesty and new hope. It is meant to dispel our confusions, to unknot their ties on us before we find ourselves entrapped in the past in ways that make a free and vigorous future impossible.

It's time, we know now, to choose between the conflicting agendas that underlie the tension. Shall we continue doing what we are doing now but do not like or shall we quit, move beyond where we are now, begin again somewhere else? Shall we maintain this relationship whatever its oppression of us or shall we end it and go on alone? Shall we admit this mistake and resolve it or continue to hide it and live for the rest of our lives in fear of its revelation? Shall we bow our heads within us in sorrow for what cannot now be changed but which lives in us still? Shall we finally accept it as an immutable lesson well learned and which every day makes us an even better person than we were before we learned it?

The choices are life-changing, yes, but internal noise indicates clearly that this life as we are living it now needs—somehow, some way—to be changed.

We are struggling with the cries of unhealed feelings and broken psyches, the pain of which drips daily into the soul. The tempest of internal turmoil keeps us tossing and turning at night, leaves us isolated from ourselves and dishonest with those who love us most. These are the things that divide the soul from itself. These are the beginnings of the schizophrenic spiritual self, the person who looks like one person to others but is entirely another within.

The major question of a person's life lies in whether or not we are willing to bring both parts of the self together—the public one and the hidden one—to stop pretending, at least to ourselves, in order to become the person we seem to be. The monastics of the desert put the problem this way: Abba Isidore of Pelusia said, "To live without speaking is better than to speak without living. For the former who lives rightly does good even by his silence but the latter does no good even when he speaks. When words and lives correspond to one another they are together the whole of philosophy."

Philosophy, the understanding of what it means to be human, to be wise, to exist in the fullness of life, is a demanding discipline. It is more than knowledge, more than simply success. It is the study of what it means to grow a crystal soul, bright and clear and true. It is that which the elimination of the pernicious noises in the soul, the coming to the fullness of the internal self, is all about. And how is that done? Our internal noises are cries for attention to the soul. Face them. Deal with them. Get help with them. Grow from them.

Without that, we are not yet fully alive.

27

THE CHALLENGE OF HOPELESSNESS

When early spiritual writers considered what would be required for a person to make progress in the spiritual life, they did not design a set of austerities. They did not make physical exercises the core of the spiritual life. They did not recommend to those who came searching for wisdom programs of rigorous fasting or sleepless nights or great penances. No, instead they recommended something far more difficult: They demanded deep, great measures of internal awareness.

They demanded that their disciples give less time to congratulating themselves on the holiness points they had achieved by ticking off religious exercises and give themselves over to the far more difficult discipline of self-knowledge. Disciples were taught to identify within themselves the spirits that colored their lives and drove their desires and moved their hearts. It was the great purifying act of being able to admit to oneself at least, what it was for which the soul pined that was making it impossible to accept the good of where they were in life. Then it was a matter of overcoming the negative impulses within so that the spirit of the joy of living in God could take them over and give them the fullness of life for which they longed.

These were not sour souls, these monastics, these truly spiritual people. Nor did they teach that the spiritual life itself was a sour enterprise. They, above all, having faced the rigors of the dry, dour desert, knew that a healthy, holy life lay within a person's own control. We are not at the mercy of the environment.

Most interesting of all, life, medicine, and psychology have in every age proved these sages true. Human beings everywhere have transcended all manner of pain. Paraplegics talk of being happy. Holocaust victims report finding God in concentration camps. People living in poverty insist they, too, find good and hope and enjoyment despite the paucity of their circumstances.

At the same time, there are people who have great health, take political freedom for granted, and live stable and comfortable lives who report their sense of hopelessness and describe lives lived in despair. To writhe for want of more than enough, to grasp for heights beyond our personal abilities to achieve them, to live in a state of perpetual dissatisfaction with life in general, as well as life in particular, is not healthy aspiration: It is the seedbed of hopelessness.

Clearly, hopelessness has at least as much to do with what we bring to life as it does with what life brings to us.

Great pain does not dampen hope and great opportunity does not ensure it. Humdrum hopelessness, the garden-variety kind of ennui or disinterest or self-doubt, comes out of our inability to take the world in hand. However small it may be. However great it may look. Hopelessness is a spiritual doldrum. It is life becalmed, without energy, without edge. It is life lived without a sense of responsibility to the rest of the world, let alone to ourselves.

What breeds hopelessness is the failure to pursue the possible in the imperfect. It is exactly those negative spirits that keep us awake at night, until we confront what we lack the courage to do, to be, to think. In Paraguay, a music teacher taught children to make musical instruments out of the glass and tin and steel in a landfill and life changed for those children. In Harlem, hope came out of playing basketball on street corners. In life in general, hope lies in taking what we have—money for the bored wealthy, education for the bored poor—and using every heartbeat within us to turn it into something worthwhile. We are required to recognize the nature of the life which we are called to live, and determine what it will take in us to accept it.

The challenge of hopelessness is the challenge to reenter the human race, to take our part in it knowing that it is as much our responsibility to shape life as it is for life to shape us. It requires us to understand that misfortune is not failure. It is at most simply a digression through life intended to make us reassess our course, our goals, our aspirations.

The paradox of hopelessness is that in it lies the invitation to get up and go on. Despite difficulties, despite the implacability of the exercise, despite the windless intervals of life, hopelessness calls us to try again, try something different, if necessary, but at least try. Hopelessness prods us to go beyond what we ourselves estimate to be our chance of succeeding. After all, who doesn't know intuitively that if we don't try, we can't possibly fail?

Most important of all, perhaps, is the possibility that hopelessness may be a sign that we have gotten ourselves into some situation far too difficult or far too foreign to our personalities or far too unrelated to who we know ourselves to really be to ever succeed at it. It's in moments like these that hopelessness calls us back to the fullness of the self and away from heights we are not meant to climb.

At the same time, hopelessness may be more about a lack of commitment than it is a lack of ability. It calls us back to our dreams and our determination to make them real. In which case, it is a call to move on, not to stay and suffer death by boredom. Albert Einstein didn't like his job at the patent office either. That didn't make him incapable of it. He simply stayed where he was but filled the remainder of his days doing what he had been born to do. On the side. In addition to. After hours. Whenever he could.

Hopelessness calls us beyond quitting what we cannot quit, to learn how to do what we have been born to do. Even if that means doing one thing while wanting to do another: math problems like Einstein, maybe; Little League athletics like everybody's favorite coaching uncle. It means going somewhere else if necessary but always to some situation where what I am able to do needs to be done. It's not a call to a job. It's a call to a life spent doing what I do best—wherever that may be, during work or after it. Einstein, after all, did most of his early groundbreaking work during the years when he could not find a university position. So he got whatever job he could, and at the same time, went on doing the math problems he loved. And that compensated for everything he couldn't do. He was happy.

When we align being able to do what we want while we do what we must, the fog of hopelessness will lift. Then we can live with the greatest degree of energy and the greatest measure of joy, however limited our resources, however many the comforts that do not content us. Then the spirits of darkness and doom lift, the feelings of hopelessness disappear. Then real life begins.

"Bloom where you are planted," the poster reads. But the poster does not tell the whole story. "Plant yourself where you know you can bloom" may well be the poster we all need to see. Or better yet, "Work the arid soil however long it takes until something that fulfills the rest of you finally makes the desert in you bloom."

28

THE COURAGE OF COWARDICE

I t's years later but I still remember the scene: He was tall and lanky, his guns slapped at his sides as he walked alone down the middle of the dusty street, his eyes fixed and cold. It was high noon. There was nowhere to hide now. The only option was to confront the enemy face-to-face and destroy him. The whole scene was the very apotheosis of righteous anger and courage, the icon of the tough, the invincible American hero.

That model has become the staple of the society. It is Mighty Mouse in action, Superman unleashed, the Terminator unbound. It is, we are to believe, the measure of manhood, the description of real maleness, the caliber of those who prefer to die rather than to give in to opposition, to the malice, to the inferior ones.

And many would call it brave. But there is another kind of courage that another equally stalwart people, both men and women, embody despite the fact that films and television programs and newspapers seldom valorize it. "It is curious," Mark Twain wrote, "that physical courage should be so common in the world and moral courage so rare."

This is the courage that refuses to become what it hates and at the same time refuses to be passive in the face of evil.

The differences between physical courage and moral courage bring the heart to a full stop. The fact is that there aren't any differences. Not really. It's just that the two differ in terms of how to achieve what they each want. Actually the two distinct postures are the same but the modern world calls one bravery and the other cowardice. The distinctions call all of us not to question courage but to discover what it really is. One type of courage is life-denying; the second type is life-giving.

The characteristics of life-denying courage as we know it are clear.

First: Whatever the cost to itself, macho courage confronts the enemy—personal or national—head-on. Let there be no doubt that this is a showdown. In this struggle, domination is the goal, superiority is the weapon of choice. This is force unlimited. We will prevail.

Second: This is a take-no-prisoners strategy. Lines are drawn and the surrender must be unconditional. There will be no space given for compromise, for dallying.

Third: The superman opponent simply refuses to enter into any kind of discussion on the merits of any other way of thinking, any other needs, any other possibilities.

This is the kind of force applied on children who have

nothing to say about the plans being made for them, nothing to say about the process of carrying them out, nothing to say about the effects those plans may have on their own dignity or degrees of life satisfaction, as well as how they may actually jeopardize it.

It is a child-beating, wife-beating, death-by-drones strategy of people with the power to work their will. It destroys the destroyable and calls that peace.

On the other hand, the characteristics of life-giving courage deal with situations where people in conflict have no desire to humiliate or vitiate others. This kind of courage does not seek to destroy opponents but to make of them comrades in righteousness.

First: Whatever the cost to itself, life-giving courage confronts enemies—personal or national—head-on. In this struggle, spiritual as well as physical survival is the goal, and integrity is the weapon of choice. So important is any issue to the people who oppose it that they will defy it to the end.

Second: However major the issue, life-giving courage resists to the end but not without attempting to negotiate the situation. There is no desire for division. Nevertheless, the resistance is total until the issues at the base of the disagreement have been resolved.

Third: Life-giving courage has no desire either to humiliate or destroy the opponent. The life-giving opponent attempts to enter into the discussion with a heart for the merits of others' perspective in mind and care for the needs of others as well as their own. This is the kind of courage that seeks to make a friend of a potential enemy.

This kind of courage is not an attempt to apply force; it is an attempt to broaden the views of those whose vision is limited.

It is the force of a boy in Tiananmen Square who faced a tank to make the point that the government would need to be willing to run down everyone in the square to end the resistance. It exposed the character of the government it confronted.

It is a win-win situation. It uses any and all means available to achieve an end that is good for everyone concerned.

It is a child-caring, person-loving, resurrection moment designed to make the powers that be responsible and responsive to everyone whose lives they affect. It is the work of people dedicated to evolution rather than revolution. Those who practice life-giving courage threaten no one but themselves with injury or death, so that those with the power to work their will can make the great life-and-death choices with integrity, with brave humility, and with common care for all the people concerned.

Both kinds of courage risk death. But life-giving resistance, as total and spiritually naked as it is, simply refuses to become what it hates.

The icons of this kind of courage are burned into our mind at least as deeply as those of gun wielders in *High Noon*.

They are Gandhi facing down the British Army on the salt march that changed Indian economic slavery.

It is women being force-fed in a Washington, D.C., jail on behalf of woman suffrage.

It is the young people in Cairo's Tahrir Square forcing

down a dictator and then forcing his successor to amend his autocracy.

They are African-American young people being beaten at a lunch counter and refusing to move, hosed in the streets and refusing to go away, chased by dogs and refusing to be cowed until desegregation came to the United States of America.

The United States saw moral character in action in African Americans who—jeered by redneck crowds, attacked by water hoses, nipped by guard dogs and threatened by armed policemen—refused to retaliate in kind. And that kind of soulfulness changed the country. It called upon the character of the white community to be just as strong and just as nonviolent. And, eventually, we became the best of ourselves because of it.

This is the courage of the Jesus who faced down the authority figures of the time over and over again, inspired by a greater law and a living God as a model to us of what it means to choose courage over cowardice.

As Hemingway writes: "Few men are willing to brave the disapproval of their fellows, the censure of their colleagues, the wrath of their society. Moral courage is a rarer commodity than bravery in battle or great intelligence. Yet it is the one essential, vital quality of those who seek to change a world which yields most painfully to change."

The question is an obvious one: When you think of all those things at night, when you find yourself struggling to decide which models of strength you yourself will practice, which looks most courageous, most brave to you?

An ancient monastic story tells of a ravaging warlord

who razed every village as he went across the land. Just the word of his coming was enough to send entire populations into the hills to live in caves until his troops passed by.

As he entered a small hamlet one day, he sneered as he said to his second-in-command, "I presume all the people have fled by this time?"

"Well, all but one old monk who refused to flee," the adjutant answered.

The commander was furious. "Bring him to me immediately," he barked.

When they dragged the old monk to the square before him, the commander screamed at him, "Do you not know who I am? I am he who can run you through with a sword and never even bat an eye."

And the old monk looked up and said, "And do you not know who I am? I am he who can let you run me through with a sword and never bat an eye."

29

THE CERTITUDE OF DOUBT

Certitude is a very tricky thing. It is so often wrong. And so often loud about it. It can be tolerated only if it comes with large doses of humility. As in, "As far as I know . . ." or "It seems to me . . ." or "Do you agree?" or a simple "I think so, but I'm not sure . . ."

Once upon a time, we were certain about the shape of the world and so allowed that belief to shape the way we dealt with the world for centuries. We thought that the world was flat, for instance, so the Greeks would not sail through the Hellespont for fear they would fall off the edge of it. Western civilization missed the existence of the East for centuries. As a result of that kind of certitude, mapmaking has always been a work in progress, always sincere and often incorrect.

We've been relentlessly certain about the inferiority of one race to another and wound up diminishing the moral quality of our own. Our Caucasian experts told us that the distance between a black man's eyes was a sure sign of his lower IQ and, after years of objective research, left the world with nothing more than the surety of how feeble their own intelligence had been.

We've been more than certain about the secondary value and the lesser intelligence of women to men and so denied ourselves the insights and talents of half the human race. But the *Irish Times* reported on its front page recently that girls were far outranking male students on their leaving cert exams there by almost fifteen points, even in subjects traditionally reserved for males.*

And on the practical level we've accepted as fact, among other things, that bloodletting was curative, that humans could not fly, that the deaf were also dumb, that cigarettes were benign and that cloning was simply beyond imagination.

As Voltaire remarked, "Doubt is not a pleasant condition, but certainty is absurd."

The problem is that certitude seduces us. It enables us to believe that what is said to be true is true because someone else said so. It simply cuts off thought. It arrests discussion in midflight. And yet we yearn for it with a passion. We spend endless, sleepless nights grappling with intellectual options in order to wiggle them into a satisfying kind of certainty without so much as a scintilla of evidence.

It is a very effective tool for kings and potentates and any powers that be. Of all the tools authority has to wield,

---

* Joe Humphreys, "Girls Beat Boys to the Honour in 50 Leaving Cert Papers," *Irish Times* (August 15, 2014).

certitude trumps them all. They call it tradition or law or infallibility, the irrefutables of any institution, the staples of fear. The timid, the insecure and the sycophants accept them without contest because they enable a people to look more pious than inept.

So rulers of all stripe and type dispense certainties—theirs—with great abandon. They do whatever it takes—define cultural dogmas, assert organizational doctrines, impose decrees, and use power, force and penal systems—to suppress the ideas of anyone who dares to question them. Ideas, after all, are dangerous things. Ideas have brought down as many myths and mysteries as they have toppled kingdoms.

Certitude carries within itself a kind of social convenience, as well. No greater conversation stopper exists than the notion that an idea is unassailable, closed to discussion, simply not open to review. "We have always done it this way; this has always been true" is authority of the most effective type. Declarations like these either end peace or spawn passivity. They make foes out of friends. Certainties turn a thinking people into a restless people, waiting for the light they know will come while watching creativity die in their midst.

But there is another way to live that runs hot and bright through darkness. There are always some in every population who know that life is not meant to be about certainty. Life, they realize, is about possibility. They see certitude as a direction but not an end.

These are the ones who understand that what we know now that is belief without proof is worthy for its own time only. At the same time, it is exactly this awareness that cows a world that prefers certitude to doubt. "How," they ask, "can anyone believe in anything when everything changes all the time?" They have no tolerance for unfinished ideas.

And yet, it is precisely the unfinished idea, however well-intentioned, that deserves the unending pursuit of the open-minded who are bent on bringing what is incomplete to the fullness of the true and the real. The real truth is that their discoveries will make life more authentic for us all.

Doubt is what shakes our arrogance and makes us look again at what we have never really looked at before. Without doubt there is little room for faith in anything. What we accept without question we will live without morality. It is in populations like this that monarchs become dictators and spiritual leaders become charlatans and knowledge becomes myth.

An ancient people tell the story of sending out two shamans to study their holy mountain so that they could know what their gods expected of them. The first shaman came back from the north side of the mountain to tell them that it was covered with fruit trees, a sign that their god would always bless them abundantly. The second shaman came back from the south side of the mountain to tell the people that it was barren and covered with rock, a sign that their god would always be with them but intended them to take care of themselves. So, which shaman was right? If both, then it is dangerous to dogmatize either position.

It is doubt, not certitude, that enables us to believe because it requires us to think deeply about an entire subject, and not simply depend on the side of reality that is on our side of the mountain. Only when we can look beyond absolutes to understand every level of life can we possibly live life to the fullest, with the deepest kind of insight, with the greatest degree of compassion for others.

Voltaire was right, of course. Certainty is comfortable but always unlikely and forever disruptive. As life changes so must our explanations and responses to it.

The absurdity of certitude is life's most seriously damaging narcotic. It accuses us of our shallowness and hollows out the soul.

Doubt is uncomfortable, yes, but doubt always leads us beyond the present moment to the kind of moments that call us to greater truth, deeper wisdom and a more adult measure of the self.

30

The Benevolence of the Unknown

Fear is the toxin of this generation. Overcrowded cities, seeping borders, professional transience, the movement of great numbers of people from one place to another on the globe like schools of fish in an aquarium, have re-created the face and nature of society. From the crowds of displaced people seeking new jobs in new places, to those being transferred from one office to another, to refugees driven from their homelands around the globe, the roads of the world are filled with strangers looking for a new home.

But the very meaning of home has changed in our time.

In the small village in which I am writing today, home is 250 families scattered across this mountainous territory where sheep are far more commonly on the roads than people. The houses are small and tucked into copses of trees or blended into the giant boulders overlooking the sea.

The only foreigners here are the "blow ins" who own small patches of land but come only seasonally, or rent holiday houses that were built to accommodate short-term tourists. Here, everyone knows everybody, at least by sight. Everyone. There are no inns, no small motels, no restaurants, no all-night coffee shops, no bus stations, no truck stops here to attract and serve transients. There could be no local home invasion by random strangers here because there are few, if any, strangers passing through. Clearly, strangers are a by-product of cities, not villages where landholdings have been in the same families for generations.

Places such as this are rare now on a planet where villages have routinely given way to large cities full of strangers and, most of all, full of people unlike ourselves. The race, religion and cultural mores of our neighbors and coworkers, our teachers and civil servants, our doctors and our children's spouses, our gardeners and our cabdrivers can't be taken for granted anymore. We are now global villages of "unlikes." It's a great moment in human history. But it is a difficult moment, as well. Even the most generous people in the world struggle, nevertheless, to understand why "they" are not "just like us." Or worse, why they don't even seem to want to be.

It is a moment rife with suspicion, prejudice, turfism, chauvinism, fear.

Suspicion is rampant. From now on, whatever goes wrong around here is because someone unlike us came along and ruined everything. We can't understand the accent so we can't get the help we need when we're shopping. The car doesn't work right, we decide, because mechanics from countries like that don't know what we're talking about when we take our vehicle to a garage. And anyway, we don't like the way they look at us. We think they're up to something.

Prejudice divides us from them and even them from themselves. We don't mind foreigners in general, we say; it's just these particular people who bother us. They should have gone somewhere where people believe in that kind of a god. We don't.

These people are everywhere now. They take our jobs, and move into our houses but don't keep them clean. Somebody has to tell them to find a place of their own.

Chauvinism evaluates everyone not like us as lesser. They don't know what it means to be a citizen here, we insist. They don't know our history. They didn't fight for this country. But they'll pull our economy down because they don't work as hard as we do.

And at the base of it all is fear. The fear of difference. The fear of otherness. The fear of loss. The fear of change. The fear of the very things that stand to make us even greater than we are. The benevolence of the unknown has escaped us. Differences, as enrichment, elude us.

Difference is the gift that unlikeness brings us. Because of our openness to differences we learn to be in the world in new and exciting ways. We learn that there is more than one kind of way to go through life and do it morally, artistically, happily. We discover that other foods are equally as good for us as anything we have become accustomed to eating. If not better. We begin to understand history and economics and even religion differently. And we encourage our children to learn other languages if they really want to be citizens of the world rather than simply its onlookers.

Differences bring us out of ourselves into a newer, fuller way of being human. We see other models of family life and begin to reexamine our own in the light of them. We begin to recognize likenesses among us that enlarge our understanding of what it means to be human beings together.

Finally, we begin to realize in blazing new ways that no particular people have a monopoly on goodness or a corner on criminal character, an option on God or an ascendancy on godlessness. We come to own that we are all simply human beings together with a great deal to learn from one another if we are ever going to be fully developed, deeply sensitive and wholly human adults. We gift the world with a new definition of home as a union of hearts rather than as a union of types.

It is, without doubt, the gifts we get from our excursions into differences—the people we come to know whom we could never have met otherwise, the wisdom we see in those we consider simpler than ourselves, the downright goodness of those we fear because we do not know them—that make us bigger of soul, greater of heart, than we could possibly ever have been otherwise.

That is the benevolence of the unknown. That is what is missing in the ghetto formation that comes from hiding in the cave of ourselves all our lives. Until we step out into the large world around us, go out of our way to meet, befriend, engage with the unknowns, we will remain forever the half of ourselves we are now. But if we move toward even one person who is our opposite, go to one country where our stereotypes have made us blind and begin to see the other as like us, the other country as a symphony of new soul, our own spirit will grow.

Antoine de Saint-Exupéry promises us the revelation that the unknown brings and the fullness of life that comes with it. "A single event," Exupéry writes, "can awaken within us a stranger totally unknown to us. To live is to be slowly born."

To be citizens of the world in a world that has itself become a global village, we must all allow ourselves to be called to life by the unknown. Then, perhaps, stunned by the sameness in us, we will no longer lose sleep worrying about the danger of immigration, the danger of strange religions, the danger that comes clothed in other colors, other accents, other ways to marry and bury and pray and be alive, all of it in the name of one humanity.

Most of all, we will all come to understand that the human race has a great deal more in common than it has differences. Then the stranger, the one totally unknown to us, the one who awakens these realizations in us, will enable us to melt into the stream of life more fully human ourselves. But first, of course, to stop the fear in the night, we must reach out. We must take into our own homes at least one other family or person because of whose differences we can come to see the ways of God in the rest of creation.

31

The Invitation of Finality

I heard of a father who never hugged his daughter good-bye without saying this blessing over her: "May every place you be make it hard for you to leave. . . . May every person you love make it hard for you to say good-bye." It takes a lot of living to really understand the pain and the beauty of that kind of blessing. To be so happy anywhere you never want to leave it, to love someone so much you cannot bear to say good-bye, must be one of God's greatest blessings. It is a life lived trailing a wake of unending happiness. It is a gift given to few.

Rather, life is made up of segments, some of them longer than others but all of them essentially freestanding, independent of the one that has gone before it. We go from childhood to adolescence to adulthood growing both physically and psychologically, moving toward what must surely be the point of human fulfillment. The temptation is to assume that at some magic number of years, at the time the society calls legal adulthood—or even retirement—that we're finished, that it's finally over, that we have reached the summit of development, that we are finally the fullness of the person we have been becoming all these beginning years.

Nothing could be further from the truth. The fact is that our lives are truly works in progress, all of them individually and at different times. We go from this to that, from here to there with only one constant: We are constantly becoming, no less at seventy-five years old than when we were four. The changes at four are predominantly, obviously, physical. The changes at seventy-five are also physical, of course, but the real changes, the great changes in us between the ages of twenty-one and eighty-five, are by then more internal than external.

One period of life follows upon another, sustained only by the spirit that is us. And in each of those periods, we stretch ourselves always toward the sun of our lives, whatever it happens to be at that moment.

Choice is the metaphor of life. We wind our way from one choice to another all the rest of our years. We choose and change and then choose again. We select this education not that education, this job not that job, this partner not that partner. We build up a scaffolding of choices, each of which, sooner or later, one way or another, ends. And then we must begin to choose all over again. One choice is a mistake, the next an achievement until, one alternative at a time, we write on our hearts the map of life we have routed for ourselves.

But not always.

The chain of choices we make for ourselves is not the whole of our life's story. They are not, often, even our most important ones.

The truth is that life's just not that neat. We make decisions every step of the way, yes, and we change many of them as time goes by. But in many instances as many things just happen as much as they are chosen. Or many of the selections we make simply evaporate even as we grasp them. What we wanted we do not get. Not because we changed them; because life changed them.

And at that point disruption sets in at the crossroad of all our plans. We are cast adrift in life with the great plan gone and nothing on the horizon to put in its place. Then, the heart cries out in the night, now what?

Loss, when it comes, is indiscriminate. It comes in many forms. A veritable viper's tangle of circumstances always. Death brings loss. I planned to move across the country until my father dies, but now someone has to stay home to look after my mother. Rejection brings loss. I wanted to work in a big city band. In fact, I was sure I'd gotten the job—until the letter came. It was a one-word answer: No. Health conditions bring loss. There's a position opening for civil volunteers in South Africa. I was accepted for it until my asthma started up again and they sent me back home. Insufficiency brings loss. I applied for a position with great promotion possibilities but they wanted credentials I did not have. A fellow five years younger than I got the job instead. Conflict brings loss. I wrote a political opinion on my Facebook page and the company fired me for identifying myself as working for them.

No doubt about it. Loss comes in many forms.

We choose, yes, but all those others are choosing, too. Their choices affect us, too. So, is life nothing more than an adult game of pickup sticks–tossed into the air helter-skelter for us to pick our way through with resignation or be felled by despair?

Not really. The Spirit of Life in us is simply richer, broader, more perceptive than we are. It takes a bevy of lost choices, it takes some experience, to come to understand that. Every choice we make for ourselves in life leaves unnoticed a number of choices we could have made. One choice cancels another. The choice we did not make represents a number of capabilities we have that this particular choice will not cultivate, a number of opportunities available that call the rest of me out of my protective shell in order to enable me to become the more of me.

The pain of one loss is always an invitation to open myself to the rest of life, to the rest of myself, to the rest of this great wide world I carry within me. Choice is still mine—only the situation has changed.

Life lies in adapting to choices that are not mine. It requires that I understand that life is not final until it ends. The space between then and now depends on choice, yes, but what I would choose to do and what is available to do are not both under my control. It is a matter of realizing that the clay of life is the clay in which I find myself. Life is not a clay I create; it is the clay I have before me at this moment to use.

It is the choice I make when unlimited choice is not an option that determines both what I do and what I am. It identifies not only what is in me but what I intend to become. Everything I choose is not the best choice I could have made, perhaps, but the way I deal with it is the choice that will define me in the end.

No, no single segment of life is final. None of them can be cast in stone. Each of them will end for some reason somewhere. But as long as everything I do and everyone with whom I share my soul represents something that when it was over I did not want to leave, I will have finally known happiness.

Those are the choices we want to make in life. Those will be the ones that really count.

Or as William Jennings Bryan put it: "Destiny is no matter of chance. It is a matter of choice. It is not a thing to be waited for, it is a thing to be achieved."

Choose wisely. May sadness be the measure of your wisdom as you go.

32

The Pain of the Search for Spiritual Painlessness

The world is an absolute marketplace of spiritual ideas now. Religion is not regional anymore. Seekers from every major tradition live within blocks of one another in every major city in the world. And in most of the small ones, as well. At one time, the very thought of such a society was unacceptable. In the United States, the integration of Catholics and Protestants was feat enough, never mind Hindus or Muslims. But those days are gone now. Great mosques and temples stand within sight of one another, even if still strange to one another, but certainly not as threats to either's integrity.

No, it's not the fear of syncretism that is at issue now—religions are not melting into one another—but, for the first period in history, they are in conversation with one another.

We are all sharing ideas, listening in to one another's debates, watching one another for signs of holiness and prodding one another for answers to the questions that keep us apart, and sharing answers in ways that bind us together. We are listening to one another's programs, going to one another's festivals, hearing one another's talk shows on radio and televisions. We are all looking everywhere for paths to the Unknown and, interestingly enough, discovering our common questions, evaluating our unique answers to them and beginning to image God from other perspectives.

Of all the things we share, the most central is not in the liturgical or theological or canonical dimensions of the religion. It is in the realm of our personal search and experience of God.

I have danced in a Sufi *fikre*, sat for hours in a Zen Buddhist tea ceremony, been part of a Hindu *puja*, attended Shabbat services in multiple Jewish synagogues, and never, in any of those moments of worship, did I doubt that these people were just as deeply involved in the search for God as I am. And that God was with us all.

And why not?

God is everywhere, they told us as children. But the question never goes away: Yes, but—where is God for me? I don't feel God. I don't hear God. I don't know how to know God. So God is surely in all these other places where the consciousness of God is also real, as well. But as much as I knew, even as a child, that it had to be true, that God was everywhere, still God was nowhere in particular in life. And, though I did not know it at the time, and so struggled through the thought of God for night after night in life, in that reality was all I needed to know about the search for God.

It was years, of course, before I realized that I was looking for Something rather than for Everything, and so I found nothing because I was looking for the wrong thing. And it is that kind of seeking that causes all the pain.

Spiritual elders in every tradition know the truth of all of that. There is no way, no trick, no strategy, no magic ritual or formula necessary to "get" God. God is already with us. We can only grow into the God who is already with us one insight, one awareness, one experience at a time. Yet, however much we sincerely seek for it, it can take years for us to sink into a perpetual sense of the presence of God.

The Sufi Sheik Ansari says of the process:
"Lashed by desire
I roamed the streets of Good and Evil
What did I gain? Nothing–
The Fire of desire grew only fiercer. . . ."

As the Sufis knew, the truth is painful: The more false starts I make, the more I want of the real thing. We seek and in seeking only want more of this God who is the magnet of our lives, the Center of our seeking. Always more.

At the same time, in the sixth century, Benedict of Nursia whose model of communal life became the model for Benedictine monasticism to this day teaches that we already have God. The "fear—the awe—of God," he says, must be "always before our eyes." We are, he tells us, to come to see the beauty and glory of God everywhere. Then, bowing down before it in our hearts, we will live in its aura. In us, around us, before us—this awareness of God is a slowly consuming process. But an ever clearer one.

So the seeker's life is a gradual sinking into the consciousness of God but, oh, the diversions along the way while we look for the trick to make it so. While we become enamored of more exciting kinds of spiritual tinsel on the way. While we look for quicker, more esoteric practices to assure ourselves that we are finally on the way.

It is a long and discouraging process, this making of the Presence of God in life some kind of magic act. When the darkness sets in and we thrash about at night looking for answers to the commonplaces of life: Where will we get the money? How can we control the child? What has happened to the relationship? We seek for God the puppeteer, God the magician, God the avenger to change the world to our designs. We tell ourselves that we are really seeking the God of Mystery and Life but we actually seek the god we have created for ourselves rather than the God of Life out of whose creative energy came our own.

When those avatars of God do not do the magic we want, or punish the people we want to punish, or change the weather and raise the stock market for us, we lose faith, we sink into the pain of abandonment—either God's abandonment of us or our abandonment of God.

We panic and begin to search in strange places, in frantic ways. We go seeking charms and spells, or we run from one temple or set of esoteric practices or saints or set of stars to another, looking for what we already have: the Presence of God who companions us through life always.

But at the heart and core of every great tradition, one

understanding is clear. We have forgotten the findings of the mystics of every religion: that God is with us. Always. That there is no reason to seek God, that now and always God is seeking us, waiting for us to respond. All we really need to do is to attend.

In that reality is all we need to know about the search for God.

In the name of God we reject whole bodies of people. In the name of God we make our god some person. For the sake of God we allow our families to be divided or abandoned or forgotten. And we call ourselves good for having done all these things. God must wince at the very thought of it.

The Hebrew Scriptures relate a story that shocked me as a child but, after years of reflection and a more open heart, gives me great hope. The story tells us that in their passion for the spiritual life—when the whole world still had only one language, were one race, one nation and were, then, capable of working together on such a great project—this people decided to dedicate themselves to the building of a great high tower. The goal was to build the tower high enough to enable them all to go up to God together. A grand design, a great model, a mighty trick, I thought. (I was in second grade, just old enough to be greatly impressed by that kind of spiritual effort in life.)

But then, the story goes on, God looked down and saw them all at work and instead of being impressed by their plan was deeply disturbed at the very sight of it. This great tower, this singular definition of one path to heaven, this foolish notion that God was available for capture made a mockery out of the very spirituality for which they sought: the awareness that God was everywhere, that God was with everyone, that God is the very Life of life. "I will confuse their language," God said, "so they cannot understand one another and I will scatter them across the world."

The story troubled me in second grade and continued to trouble me for years. What kind of a God was it who would not want people to reach the top of their tower to find God? And then I realized what was going on in the story. Without a common language anymore and dispersed across the world, they would all have to be open to learning from one another about the nature and presence of God in life. Otherwise, they would always think that their one experience and perspective and relationship was all there was to know about God.

It is a story more important now, I think, than ever before.

The spiritual life is a very personal thing. All of life is its teacher. No one has all of it at any one time and everyone has some of it always. Indeed, we all have God but melting into the presence and heart of God takes great contemplation, conscious effort, total immersion and the willingness to give up our own ideas of God. Clearest of all is the fact that each and all the traditions of all the ages and all the people we will ever meet have something to teach us about it. That takes a lifetime of listening, of living, of suffering the pain of the process and the pain of the distance.

Eddie Cantor once said, "It took me twenty years to become an overnight success." In the end we will certainly succeed.

ACKNOWLEDGMENTS

I did not realize until I sat down to write these acknowledgments just how difficult it would be. This book is about what it takes to live well in the prevailing atmosphere of contemporary social life. It has no scientific answers to provide because these are not scientific issues. These are issues of the soul, of the overworked mind, of the hurting heart, of the overwrought life.

The fact is that this has been a very different kind of book. Its ideas can't be "proven" statistically, though the statistics on their existence are surely close to universal. They can't be pronounced on morally, though they surely tax the moral latitudes of every level of life. They are untreatable in psychological terms, though they are undoubtedly part of every conversation about what both strains or enhances an individual's emotional balance.

So to all these friends and colleagues I owe a special note of thanks for their interest and for their assurance that the work engaged them in rethinking their own lives, as

ACKNOWLEDGMENTS

well as in the evaluation of the clarity and niceties of the writing.

I acknowledge my editors at Random House, then, with special gratitude. They saw this book through from beginning to end. Gary Jansen and Amanda O'Connor have given this small volume devoted to the conundrums of contemporary life at least as much attention as is customarily given to tomes of history and the great ideas of modern science twice its size. Their commitment to beginning this conversation on what it takes to be human, a human being today is itself a sign of the importance of what is obvious but unspoken in society. Their careful concern for every step of the process has given this project depth and quality beyond its size.

The bank of readers who reviewed the manuscript before its final draft were invaluable, too, not just because they read the text but because they confirmed the notion that the topics treated in this book are, indeed, the underlying issues of modern life. Too much noise, too much isolating silence, too little privacy, too much sense of being alone even in the midst of the suffocating crowds—among all the other omnipresent but unspoken dimensions of life—are so common to modern life. And clearest of all, perhaps, is the need to be able to talk all of these things out with someone who feels the same.

Each of these readers made a special contribution that strengthened the text, of course. But, most of all, they confirmed the value of the topics. They made the struggle to find ways of dealing with these truths worth the effort. I am particularly indebted to Kelly Adamson, Gail

Grossman Freyne, Sara Pitzer, Kathy Schatzberg and Ann Michaud, OSB.

I am, as usual, especially indebted to the team of Benedictine Sisters who make it possible for me to write while they deal with all the day-to-day at the office. They handle all the regular tasks in addition to tasks dealing with the manuscript preparation and the editorial demands that make it possible to present a book to the public, all the while knowing that you have done everything to make it possible for other equally serious readers to make it worth their while to enter this conversation of the human soul.

To them I am forever grateful for this very real contribution to the writing art. Without them as a team, none of this would ever have been possible. Mary Lou Kownacki, OSB, is an editorial sounding board of unequaled depth. Maureen Tobin, OSB, is a personal assistant and office manager of invaluable personal concern and wisdom. She makes the world go round when I get off of it to write. Susan Doubet, OSB, is the mind behind the mind. She scours the files, checks every word, every number, every date, every phone call from every editor, and every reference. And then, after all of that, is still good enough to tell me what doesn't make sense, however correct it might be.

And finally, to you the reader, who will assess and discuss and arm wrestle these ideas to the ground of the spirit, I am indebted for your contribution to the public discourse on what it means to be a thinking, feeling, fully alive human being.